Spiritual Survival in the Modern World

Spiritual Survival in the Modern World

Insights from C. S. Lewis's
Screwtape Letters

Andrew Dean Swafford

WIPF & STOCK · Eugene, Oregon

Wipf & Stock
An Imprint of Wipf and Stock Publishers
199 W. 8th Ave., Suite 3
Eugene, OR 97401

www.wipfandstock.com

PAPERBACK ISBN: 978-1-4982-9520-8
HARDCOVER ISBN: 978-1-4982-9522-2
EBOOK ISBN: 978-1-4982-9521-5

Manufactured in the U.S.A.   11/17/16

To my wife, Sarah,
and our four children, Thomas, Fulton, Cate, and Kolbe

Contents

Contents

Acknowledgments

I WOULD LIKE TO thank my wife for her suggestions to the manuscript—it certainly improved under her watch.

I would also like to acknowledge the wonderful students at Benedictine College; their insightful comments and questions over the years in reading through *Screwtape Letters* together has certainly enhanced this project.

And lastly, thanks of course goes to Almighty God—in whom we live and breathe and have our very being.

A Letter to the Reader

I HAVE BEEN A professor of theology for ten years now at Benedictine College in Atchison, Kansas, and for the past several years I have taught a class called "Christian Moral Life." When I first taught it, almost on a whim, I decided to add a C. S. Lewis component to the course, reading through *The Screwtape Letters*, *The Great Divorce*, and *Mere Christianity* with my students.

From the very beginning, I was struck by how so many of my students responded to Lewis—students from all different faith backgrounds (even those with no faith background at all) took to him in a deep and personal way. They were moved by how well Lewis explained key psychological realities, or how in such a succinct manner he could get at the core of the spiritual and moral life. In short, Lewis consistently made them want to be a better person. And *Screwtape Letters*, especially, has been a constant favorite of theirs.

This experience—over several years with so many different kinds of students—has led to the writing of this book. In short, I wanted to share with you what so many of my students have enjoyed so much. I hope you'll find it as empowering and eye-opening as they have.

Now for an introductory sense of what this book is about: *Screwtape Letters* are thirty-one fictional letters written by a demon named Screwtape; these letters are addressed to Screwtape's nephew, Wormwood. The content of these letters are Screwtape's advice to Wormwood on how to seduce the human being over whom Wormwood has demonic charge. In other words, Wormwood is the demonic equivalent of a guardian angel and has been assigned to a particular human being—a man in our case, also referred to as Wormwood's "patient." So, we have three main characters: Screwtape (uncle demon and author of the letters), Wormwood (nephew demon and recipient of the letters), and the patient (the man whom Wormwood is trying to seduce and bring to hell). Throughout the book, Screwtape also refers to the "Enemy," by which he means God.

As might be expected, Screwtape's letters range the entire gamut of human life—touching on everything from prayer, relationships, friendships, suffering, anxiety, despair, love, virtue, sarcasm, and so much more. We won't discuss every letter, but we will treat them in the order in which they appear in C. S. Lewis's book. Thus, while some common themes do emerge, some of the book will seem a bit disjointed every now and then; the reason is because Screwtape's counsel ranges so far and wide. But they are all united in that they show us—through seemingly every facet of life—how the devil seeks to bring about our downfall. What unites the book, then, is our unraveling of Screwtape's advice with the express purpose of putting together our own modern-day spiritual survival guide. Though he writes as a demon, Screwtape understands things surprisingly well, often grasping God's vantage point far better than the human patient—indeed, far better than we typically do. It's that keen demonic insight that—when untwisted—will be our guiding light.

We're in this together—be assured of my prayers,

Dr. Andrew Swafford

Chapter 1

Letter 3: Domestic Hatred

WE BEGIN THE STORY in letter 3, where the patient has just recently become a Christian. What is so striking about this particular letter is that we see here the paramount importance of the "little things"—that the dramatic battle of each of our lives is very often won or lost in the day-to-day, in the ordinariness of life. For Lewis, such events are far more important in our walk with Christ than we realize. As spiritual writer Jacques Philippe puts it, "The first steps on the ladder of sanctity could very well be those of my own apartment."[1]

The patient is living with his mother and Screwtape advises Wormwood to stir up "domestic hatred" between the two, by which he means the typical family strife that often erodes bonds within a family.[2] In the story, the man has just begun to take his Christian faith seriously, while the aging mother is a nominal Christian at best. Needless to say, they are not on the same page and there is tension between the two.

Being Preoccupied

Screwtape advises Wormwood to keep the patient's mind focused on the "inner life," both with regard to himself as well as his mother. What this means in practice is that his attention will be continually turned inward, making him less and less concerned with loving-kindness toward his mother; and when he thinks of his mother,

1. Philippe, *Searching for and Maintaining Peace*, 82.
2. Lewis, *Screwtape Letters*, 13.

1

he'll be focused on her inner *spiritual* life (or lack thereof) and will therefore be less and less compassionate with regard to her *physical* suffering (which happens to be rheumatism). Screwtape writes, "Keep his mind off the most elementary duties by directing it to the most advanced and spiritual ones."[3] This sounds paradoxical, but it is deceptive for that very reason: the more the man concentrates on himself and the growth of his own inner sentiments, the more he misses the obvious—namely, the charity Christ expects of him for those immediately in his care—in this case, his mother. Screwtape explains:

> You must bring him to a condition in which he can practice self-examination for an hour without discovering any of those facts about himself which are perfectly clear to anyone who has ever lived in the same house with him or worked in the same office.[4]

As is so often our experience, the people right in front of us are those who most easily "push our buttons"; they are the people we find it most difficult to love on a consistent basis. After all, where do we "let our hair down"—at home or at work? Usually, we put on a happy face at work and all too often give the worst version of ourselves to our families.

The man's focus on his interior life—even his perceived interior growth—ironically hinders him from actively living out these Christian virtues; in other words, a theme throughout this book is that the demonic strategy is to get us <u>focused on ourselves</u>—*preoccupied with ourselves*—as opposed to turning outward in love of God and neighbor. This makes us spiritually narcissistic and less and less available to those around us—making us less and less free to love.

As we'll see, the Christian life is one in which we "forget" ourselves—our egos, desires, ambitions, fears, and insecurities—and concentrate more and more outwardly on love of God and neighbour, thereby becoming less and less self-absorbed. Thus, the

3. Ibid., 11.
4. Ibid., 12.

Christian life enables us to enter more fully into the lives of those around us.

We know what it feels like when this doesn't happen—when we feel like the person with whom we are speaking is not "really" listening; they can't get past their daily tasks or concerns and truly enter into our world. For to truly enter into the world of another— asking someone how they're doing and really being concerned with their genuine response—is not all that common, we know how painful it is when it doesn't happen. This is why it's such a tremendous act of Christ-like charity to put our own concerns aside and sincerely enter the experience of the other. And perhaps nowhere is this more difficult to do on a consistent basis than in the context of everyday family life.

For Screwtape, directing the man's focus in prayer on his mother's inner life keeps his attention fixed on her perceived *in- adequacies*—and not on her physical ailments—cultivating more and more frustration with her, and less and less pity for her painful condition. Screwtape writes: "Make sure that they [his prayers] are always very 'spiritual', that he is always concerned with the state of her soul and *never with her rheumatism.*"[5] This will have the effect of keeping his mind on "her sins"—by which "he can be induced to mean any of her actions which are inconvenient or irritating to himself."[6]

Notice how the man's ego has become the barometer of good and evil, the measuring stick of his mother's "sins." This is the re- sult of the turn to self: everything is measured by how it makes me feel; there is no room left for a sincere concern for the other—only for how it affects me. That is, there is no room for genuine love.

Domestic Hatred

Screwtape then turns to the dynamics of living together. When we're on a mission trip, or a retreat (both of which are extremely

5. Ibid., emphasis added.
6. Ibid.

good in themselves!), we tend to perceive directly that we are living the Christian life; we are moving in the right direction and growing closer to our Lord. But as mentioned above, our real mettle—the heart of our character—is very often tested the most right where we live, in the ordinariness of day-to-day life.

I have known countless students over the years who have had dramatic conversions to Christ; and surrounded by fellow Christians at the college, they are on fire and thriving; but when they go home, they find themselves out of place and disappointed with the lack of fervor in their own families. I tell them that some of their biggest and most important battles will be fought at home; this is where the devil will test us the most—but this is also where we often least expect it and are therefore least prepared.

I often tell my students that this won't go away when they are married. They tend to have a sense that they'll meet another fervent Christian and the two of them will prayerfully live a Christian marriage of bliss and happiness, having none of the problems of "unbelievers." What they are often unprepared for is the real human dynamic of marriage and family life. In their ministries and apostolates, or in their secular professional life, lots of people will tell them how great they are and how wonderful they're doing. But such is seldom the case in the nitty-gritty of family life—of changing diapers and paying bills, of compromise and making hard decisions.

When you get down to the brass tacks of living together in married life, you see what someone is really made of from the inside out. I often tell my students that *marriage is when your spouse will see you at your worst and love you through it.* And this is the beauty of committed married love. But this doesn't give us a "pass" to give our spouses our worst; we should give them our very best, and the practice of giving our best doesn't grow up overnight; rather, the habits we form in the day-to-day eventually become the norm for us, as is the case with any athlete practicing a certain craft or skill. After all, what do coaches constantly say?—*you play how you practice.* In this sense, practice makes—if not perfect—more and more *permanent.*

Screwtape (unwittingly) shows us the importance of growing in the human skills and Christian charity necessary to live such basics of family life well—to allow Christ to transform our entire lives, the public aspect as well as that behind the scenes. Here we see that the day-to-day battles of ordinary life are far more important than we realize, both in Christ's eyes *and* in the demonic strategy to bring us down.

So what is "domestic hatred" more concretely? While we will continue to discuss it throughout the rest of this chapter, Screwtape captures its thrust here: "When two humans have lived together for many years it usually happens that each has tones of voice and expressions of face which are almost unendurably irritating to the other."[7] Accordingly, regarding the patient, Screwtape instructs:

> Let him assume that *she* [his mother] *knows how annoying it is and does it to annoy*—if you know your job [speaking to Wormwood] he will not notice the immense improbability of the assumption. And, of course, never let him suspect that he has tones and looks which similarly annoy her.[8]

Negative Interpretation

Notice Screwtape's attempt to cultivate the man's perception that his mother does such things *on purpose*, just to irritate him. In a wonderful book on Christian marriage, *Lasting Promise*, the authors discuss several negative patterns in marriage which, in their counseling experience, have shown themselves to be the best indicators of future marital problems and divorce.[9]

One of these negative patterns is called "*negative interpretation*," which occurs when one partner casts the actions and motives of the other in a more negative and malicious light than they really are. They point out that once a negative interpretation

---

7. Lewis, *Screwtape Letters*, 13.

8. Ibid, emphasis added.

9. Stanley et al., *Lasting Promise*, 26-49.

becomes strong enough, there is really nothing that the other person can do to overcome it.[10] No matter what the other person says or does, their actions will be read through a negatively charged lens, coloring their motives in a way *that confirms their partner's pre-existing narrative.* This obviously sets up a negatively charged environment, brimming with tension and set to boil over whenever the right trigger presents itself—a trigger that in itself may not be all that significant; but against the backdrop of such a charged environment, it becomes nothing short of explosive.

What the authors recommend is as simple as it is difficult to live up to: first, realize that your partner's motives are usually good or neutral (seldom are they are actually malicious); and second, *actively look for evidence to the contrary.*[11] That is, make a concerted effort to look for evidence of good will from your partner that contradicts your negative assumptions. So often we simply see what we want to see; we select evidence from our partner's behavior that confirms our pre-existing narrative, ignoring the rest. And as this continues, we hold our partner prisoner to the past, *always projecting the past upon the present.* In such a spiral of events, our partner can't break the cycle and the joy of married life is thereby snuffed out. And of course, this dynamic readily occurs in other relationships as well (e.g., roommates, siblings), so this counsel is widely applicable.

The Double Standard

In the following, Screwtape gives us a fuller account of what he means by "domestic hatred." I think just about every family in the country can relate to this experience, but we seldom recognize its diabolical and demonic undercurrent—that is, we seldom realize just how important such moments really are. Screwtape writes:

> In civilized life domestic hatred usually expresses itself
> by saying things which would appear quite harmless on

---

10. Ibid., 36-7.
11. Ibid., 40.

paper (the *words* are not offensive) but in such a voice, or
at such a moment, that they are not far short of a blow
in the face.[12]

As we see here, it's not the words per se, but the *way* they're
said (or their *timing*) that transforms a supposedly innocuous
phrase into a verbal dagger. And then the instigator defends himself or herself *only with respect to the words*, while the other person
reacts not to the words themselves but to the words *interpreted
in their fullest and most sensitive context, taking into account their
unspoken and hurtful intent*. Since the two parties are pointing to
slightly different things—the *words themselves* or their *charged
tone and context*—Screwtape recommends cultivating a "double
standard" of sorts, one sure to keep tensions high and the emotional connection between the two almost non-existent:

> To keep this game up you and Glubose [the mother's
> "guardian" demon] must see to it that each of these two
> fools has a sort of double standard. Your patient must de-
> mand that all his own utterances are to be taken at their
> face value *and judged simply on the actual words*, while *at
> the same time judging all his mother's utterances with the
> fullest and most over-sensitive interpretation of the tone
> and context and the suspected intention*.[13]

So, one party makes their defense based upon the words
alone, while the other reacts angrily to the words taken in their
fullest and most over-sensitive context. This is of course a recipe
for disaster—but, interestingly, a disaster in which *both parties can
walk away feeling fully justified, totally uncomprehending as to how
the other can fail to see it the same way*! Sound familiar? It certainly
does to me. Screwtape continues:

> She [his mother] must be encouraged to do the same to
> him. Hence from every quarrel they can both go away
> convinced, or very nearly convinced, that they are quite
> innocent. You know the kind of thing: "I simply ask what

12. Lewis, *Screwtape Letters*, 13.
13. Ibid., 14.

time dinner will be and she flies into a temper." Once this habit is well established you have the delightful situation of a human saying things *with the express purpose of offending and yet having a grievance when offence is taken.*[14]

Steps Toward a Solution

Once one falls into these ruts—with siblings, roommates, parents, or spouses—it becomes harder and harder to break the cycle; it becomes a <u>pattern of dysfunction</u> which one easily falls into, since it doesn't take much for one person to light the fuse, leading to exchanges like the above. The only way to thwart such a cycle is either to stop it before it starts or to have the strength to defuse (and not escalate) the situation once it has begun.[15] But to do either is to be led by right reason and Christian charity, not simply raw emotion—that is, one must have the strength to rise above one's spontaneous emotional reaction in the moment and choose the higher path of love. This takes great strength, and in certain moments it is nothing short of heroic.

This is exactly what virtue is all about—being led by right reason and not simply dominated by emotion. Easier said than done, I know, but that's why it's so important to develop good *habits*; for eventually we settle into *patterns* based upon our habitual ways of reacting to various situations—we want to strengthen good habits and curb bad ones. And here, we begin to see the intimate connection between virtue—good habits—and a happy and joyful life.[16]

We know that children do what feels good; children are dominated by their desires and emotions and that's why they throw tantrums. Maturation is very much about the attainment of self-control and the ability to do what needs to be done regardless of how one feels. Deep down, we know this; and generally, for most

14. Ibid, emphasis added.

15. See Stanley et al., *Lasting Promise*, 29–32. "Escalation" is also one of the negative patterns that the authors suggest is a major indicator for future marital problems.

16. See my *John Paul II to Aristotle and Back Again*, 23–31.

of our lives, we live this out accordingly—or else we wouldn't be able to hold down a job, finish school, or play on a competitive sports team.

But we tend to forget such basics when it comes to family life. That is, in the home, we often let our guard down, responding here or there with a snappy tone we would never dream of using elsewhere. In these moments, we are letting our emotions get the best of us, often leading to verbal jousting matches with family members, with the express purpose of scoring points by wounding the other. Sometimes such bouts are less conspicuous and the attacks less overt, often resorting to sarcasm or passive-aggressive comments; either way, we know from experience that such wounds hurt—and over time, they corrode our communion with one another.

Perhaps we let our guard down because we know that our family will still love us; and we don't act in such a manner outside the home precisely because we *don't assume* that our coworkers will love us unconditionally. No doubt, this is largely true, but the beauty of such unconditional love in the home is not an excuse for taking things out on our family or roommates.

What if we changed our mental framework a bit? What if we assumed upfront that our most important battles—our most important spiritual struggles for Jesus—were those that occur right in the home every day? We tend to fall on our faces here because for some reason we think home life should be easy, or that we get an automatic pass because it's family. And since we tend to assume work life should be hard, we walk into the office prepared to give our very best to those around us.

From Screwtape, we can take away the fact that home life is the real stage upon which our spiritual war is waged. And in fact, as St. John Paul II used to say quite frequently, the *"family is the cell of society"* and *"civilization passes by way of the family."* Society will only be as strong as our families; and strong families stem not just from passing on the Christian faith in catechetical form, but from living out the Christian life *joyfully* together; this makes it *attractive* to the next generation—it shows us the peace the world cannot give (see John 14:27).

With Christ and over time, such small things can change the course of a child's life, a marriage, and even society at large. Indeed, the real battle of our lives is fought in the little things, when very few are watching; the size of the audience has no bearing on the spiritual magnitude of what is actually taking place, a point Screwtape sees quite clearly.

In our next chapter, we turn to prayer, and we'll notice there as well that Screwtape seeks to employ the ordinary in order to bring about our destruction—indeed, here to bring us to despair.

Chapter 2

Letters 8 and 9: Avoiding Despair

IN THIS CHAPTER, WE move from domestic strife and our need to counteract it, to the great difficulty of persevering in prayer. Anybody who has spent any time trying to live a life of discipleship knows that our walk with Christ—like our family life—is marked by highs and lows.

Screwtape refers here to what he calls the "law of undulation," by which he means the ups and downs that humans experience in any endeavor—including prayer. The reason is because "humans are amphibians"; that is, "half spirit and half animal."[1] Our spirit reaches for the constancy of eternity, while our bodies are subject to time and change—moods that go up and down. And this is the *normal* course of things. Screwtape explains:

> As spirits they belong to the eternal world, but as animals they inhabit time. This means that while their spirit can be directed to an eternal object, their bodies, passions, and imaginations are in continual change, for to be in time means to change. Their nearest approach to constancy, therefore, is undulation—the repeated return to a level from which they repeatedly fall back, a series of troughs and peaks.[2]

If we are unaware of this general law—the ebb and flow of human life, the normal ups and downs—we will be surprised and taken aback when the low period (the trough) hits. We won't recognize it as a trough *period*—that is, as a *season*—rather, we will tend to see it as something that has gone wrong *permanently.*

1. Lewis, *Screwtape Letters*, 37.
2. Ibid.

These low periods, then, attempt to take psychological control over our past and future. In other words, in a trough period one feels far from God and prayer has lost its appeal. This experience tends to cast its shadow backward over our previous spiritual history: we wonder whether our past conversion and encounter with God was even real; we are haunted by the thought that perhaps it was all a figment of our imagination. And it casts its shadow forward as well: in these dark moments, the worst part is often the subtle insinuation that it will last forever.[3]

From Screwtape's vantage point, therefore, it's best if the human patient has no notion that the trough period is normal; if the patient is unaware of the law of undulation—the normal ebb and flow of troughs and peaks—then the trough period will put him on his back unexpectedly, claiming psychological tyranny over the patient's spiritual past, present, and future—bringing about a suffering that, as we know, can become literally unbearable.

Exploiting the Trough Period

In the context of letter 8, Screwtape chides Wormwood for gloating over the patient's spiritual dryness, since dryness of itself does *not*, according to Screwtape, favor the demonic side. He writes:

> The dryness and dullness through which your patient is now going are not, as you fondly suppose, your workmanship; they are merely a natural phenomenon which will do us no good *unless you make a good use of it.*[4]

Thus, the spiritual trough period does not inherently favor the side of the demons: it must be "properly exploited"[5] if it's going to reap demonic fruit.

Man cannot live without joy, and if we can't find it spiritually, we often turn to other outlets—this is what *comfort food* is all

---

3. These issues are treated further in the appendix, summarizing St. Ignatius of Loyola's teaching on overcoming desolation.

4. Lewis, *Scewtape*, 38, emphasis added.

5. Ibid., 43.

about. We're spiritually depressed, so we often turn to a physical pick-me-up. Whether it's food, pornography, sex, excessive gambling, or alcohol, sometimes these things are sought out of a deep spiritual restlessness, a deep sorrow and lack of fulfillment and meaning in one's life.

For this reason, the first way Screwtape instructs Wormwood to exploit the trough period is through "sensual temptations."[6] For Screwtape, when one feels close to God and spiritually fulfilled, we are more immune to such attacks; but when one is down, a spiritual attack of this kind has more chance of success.[7]

But for Screwtape, an even *better* way to exploit the trough period is "*through the patient's own thoughts about it.*"[8] Here, Screwtape prefers despair to sensual sins.

The first goal for Screwtape is again to ensure that the patient has no awareness of the law of undulation—no awareness that the trough period is normal.[9] Unaware of this general law, he is bound to think that something has gone seriously wrong when it does occur. Screwtape writes:

> Do not let him suspect the law of undulation. Let him assume that the first ardors of his conversion might have been expected to last, and ought to have lasted forever, *and that his present dryness is an equally permanent condition.*[10]

As we have said, this is how the devil often takes hold of us— by getting us to forget that life has its *seasons*. And again, perhaps the hardest part of any spiritual or psychological suffering is the feeling that this spiritual bondage will last forever—this is what often makes it unbearable.

But if we know that life has its seasons, then we'll be more able to realize that a bad day, a bad week, or even a bad month is

6. Ibid.

7. Ibid., 43–44. "The attack [sensual temptation] has a much better chance of success when the man's whole inner world is drab and cold and empty."

8. Ibid., 45, emphasis added.

9. Ibid.

10. Ibid.

not a bad life—our spiritual winter will eventually turn to spring and summer.

Indeed, in believing this we have already begun to break the chains of despair and doubt—precisely because the fierceness of their grip lay in the notion that they will last forever. The very moment we choose not to believe this, the darkness of night begins to give way to the dawn of day. This is why some spiritual writers, in fact, urge us to believe—in the midst of desolation—that consolation will return *soon*. This sounds spiritually bold and provocative, but the very act of choosing to believe this already starts to reverse the psychological trajectory of the downward spiral.[11]

The Irresistible and the Indisputable

As Screwtape said earlier, the trough period must be properly exploited. In fact, he actually warns Wormwood that the Enemy (God) makes *more* use of troughs than he does peaks! Screwtape writes:

> Now it may surprise you to learn that in His efforts to get permanent possession of a soul, He [the Enemy, i.e., God] relies on the troughs even more than on the peaks; some of His special favorites have gone through longer and deeper troughs than anyone else.[12]

What does Screwtape mean here? Is it really the case that God utilizes the trough period, *even more than the peak period*, to make human persons into the kind of creatures he desires?

Screwtape goes on to explain that the Enemy refuses to use the "*Irresistible*" and the "*Indisputable*."[13] Indeed, this is why faith is a *virtue.* (Many of us have often wondered about the "hiddenness" of God—why doesn't he show himself to the world in an *indisputable* way? Why doesn't he show himself to *me* in a more obvious way?)

---

11. See this teaching further expounded in the appendix.

12. Ibid., 38.

13. Ibid., 39.

As Peter Kreeft once said, in terms of evidence for God, "He gave us *enough.*" That is, God didn't leave us completely in the dark; but he doesn't overwhelm us with evidence either. In Kreeft's words, "He gave us enough." This is fitting since God desires our free choice of him in love; if he overwhelmed us with evidence—if he gave us the *indisputable* and the *irresistible*—it might take away our ability to *choose* him in love; that is, it might coerce us, as it were. Screwtape explains:

> Merely to override a human will . . . would be for Him useless. He cannot ravish. He can only woo. . . . He is prepared to do a little overriding at the beginning. He will set them off with communications of His presence which, though faint, seem great to them, with emotional sweetness and easy conquest over temptation. But he never allows this state of affairs to last long. Sooner or later He withdraws, if not in fact, at least from their conscious experience, all those supports and incentives. He leaves the creature to stand up on its own . . .[14]

For Screwtape (and for Lewis), this process *matures* our love for God. In any romance there is a "honeymoon period" of excitement—and so it is with God. But in the deepening of that love, the roots must go beyond mere excitement. And as the roots deepen, the emotional experience actually grows richer and deeper, but not without the trial of experiencing the superficial sweetness wane. These are the "growing pains" of love.

In the spiritual life, when the creature begins to seek God for his own sake—and not just the sweetness of the emotional experience—the person's love for God begins to really grow. And at this point, when a person perseveres here, Screwtape recognizes that his own cause is most in jeopardy:

> Our cause is never more in danger than when a human, no longer desiring, but still intending, to do our Enemy's will, looks round upon a universe from which every trace

---

14. Ibid., 39–40.

of Him seems to have vanished, and asks why he has been forsaken, *and still obeys.*[15]

Lessons Drawn

In sum, if we're simply aware that ups and downs are the normal course of things, we are infinitely more prepared to handle the adversity when it comes. Indeed, when things are going well, we should maintain something of an even keel attitude, realizing that this peak will eventually give way to a trough. And likewise, when a trough period comes along, we need to realize that it too is a season—and as a season, it will not last forever.[16]

If we can discern these movements as they're happening, we will be more able to rise above our spontaneous and emotional reactions—whether good or bad. That is, in a high moment, first, we should enjoy it; but second, we should reflect on the fact that it will not last forever—that is, we should *prepare* for the adversity that will eventually come.[17]

One way we can do this is to commit *now* in our minds and hearts not to buy into the lies that will come into our heads when the trough period approaches. That is, in the spiritual trough, we will "forget" God's love for us; we will "forget" our encounters with God—the times we felt so close to him—and we may assume that such encounters were not "real," that perhaps God isn't even real. In the high period, we need to preemptively reflect on this temptation and commit to holding onto—and not forgetting—our real encounter with God. In the high period, we need to realize that a down period will eventually follow and that the psychological experiences described above are likely to be part of it. Again, the way in which the devil will chiefly tempt us when we are down is "through our own thoughts about it"[18]—thoughts that crush us

15. Ibid., 40, emphasis added.
16. This point is developed further in the appendix.
17. Again, see the appendix for more on this thought.
18. Ibid., 45.

and lead us to despair, as they attempt to redefine our spiritual past and take control of our future.

But if we know this ahead of time, we will be more apt to name it and claim it when it happens. That is, if we realize (before it occurs) that this is the normal ebb and flow of human life, we'll be more able to recognize what is happening spiritually and psychologically, and thereby be more equipped to rise above our spontaneous emotional reaction in the midst of it and see it clearly for what it is—namely, a *season*.

If we can discern what is happening in the midst of the trough, we will have already broken much of its grip; for as we have said, its power lay in (1) *taking us by surprise* and (2) its insinuation that *it will last forever*. If we can recognize it for what it is in the moment, we have already come to a glimpse of hope, since we'll realize both that it's *normal* and that *it won't last forever*. At that moment, the spiritual captive is being set free.

Finally, as Screwtape suggested above, even in the trough period, God is at work in us. In Screwtape's own words, "*It is during such trough periods, much more than during the peak periods, that it is growing into the sort of creature He wants it to be.*"[19] If we have a sense for God's providence in and through the *trough* period—that he is stretching us in order that we may grow—this too makes it easier to bear. In other words, part of the incredible suffering of the trough period is its apparent *meaninglessness*. But if we choose to believe that God is still at work in our lives, even in and through our spiritual troughs, then we will begin to see some meaning in it—and from meaning comes hope.

People can go through much suffering when there is meaning attached to it—just look at the life of any serious athlete, student, musician, or artist. But when the sense of meaning and purpose is lost, even the smallest suffering becomes unbearable. Realizing—even if it doesn't feel like it—that God is mysteriously at work in the midst of our spiritual trough dramatically changes our outlook, and helps to make our psychological and spiritual malaise much more endurable.

19. Ibid., 40, emphasis added.

17

God is the potter and we are clay, and he is shaping us into his masterpieces; and he uses all kinds of instruments to bring this about—often ones we wouldn't choose ourselves. But we tend not to see the impact of such trough periods and the growth they have brought about until *after* we have come through the other side and reflect back upon it.

For this reason, when we are in a trough period, it is helpful to reflect on how we have grown through *previous* trough periods. This helps to give us a sense of meaning and purpose *in the midst of the present darkness*, stirring hope that this trough period will likewise yield future growth. Again, kindling this sense of meaning and purpose dramatically loosens the grip of despair.

In the next chapter, the patient encounters a new stage in his life—he has met a new group of friends. While Screwtape seeks to use these friends to bring the patient down, we will take the occasion to explore more fully how we can better evangelize those around us—by simply being ourselves.

Chapter 3

Letter 10: Real Authenticity

AT THIS POINT IN the narrative, the patient has made a new set of friends—worldly friends whom Screwtape seeks to utilize in the seduction of the patient.

Screwtape sees in this encounter a "subtle betrayal," which he seeks to exploit; that is, the patient wants to fit in with his new friends, and in doing so he is not fully himself. He does not denounce his faith openly, but subtly conceals his Christian faith—in such a way that the patient himself perceives this as no big deal; but for Screwtape, there is much more going on than meets the eye:

> There is a subtle play of looks and tones and laughs by which a mortal can imply that he is of the same party as those to whom he is speaking. That is the kind of betrayal you should especially encourage, because the man does not fully realize it himself; *and by the time he does, you will have made withdrawal difficult.*[1]

Notice Screwtape's observation that the longer the patient hides his true self, the harder it will be to come clean and be real in the future. And again, there is no notion of open denial—from Screwtape's vantage point, the goal is simply to "postpone" any open acknowledgment:

> No doubt he must very soon realize that his own faith is in direct opposition to the assumptions on which all the conversation of his new friends is based. I don't think that matters much provided that you can persuade him to postpone any open acknowledgment of the fact, and

1. Lewis, *Screwtape Letters*, 49–50, emphasis added.

this, with the aid of shame, pride, modesty and vanity, will be easy to do. As long as the postponement lasts he will be in a false position. *He will be silent when he ought to speak and laugh when he ought to be silent.*[2]

I'm sure we've all been in situations before where an off-colored joke was told or some comment given that made us feel a bit uncomfortable—something was said that we certainly did not approve of, but we didn't quite know how to react. And how do we typically respond? Often, with a little nervous laughter of our own. That's in part what Screwtape means by being "silent" when we "ought to speak," and "laughing" when we "ought to be silent."

From Screwtape's vantage point, the longer we pretend to be something we're not, the more our new mode of life shapes us; in other words, the more central this new friend group becomes to our lives, the more we'll actually become the person we're posing as—in Screwtape's words, "All mortals tend to turn into the thing they are pretending to be."[3]

Evangelization and Being Ourselves

The irony in letter 10 is that the patient isn't really being authentic and honest with anyone. In a sense, he is even betraying his new friends; and to this extent, his new friendships are not only superficial, but based on a lie.

As Screwtape recounts, it is the patient's vanity that makes possible a twofold betrayal: though the patient is trying to fit in with his secular friends, he actually looks down upon them, since *he* is privy to a spiritual world of which they are ignorant—he has a deeper side which they lack. And though the patient is still going to church, he also looks down upon his simpleton church friends, who couldn't possibly understand the sophisticated secular world beyond their horizons. Screwtape explains:

2. Ibid., 50, emphasis added.
3. Ibid.

This is done by exploiting his vanity. He can be taught to enjoy kneeling beside the grocer on Sunday just because he remembers the grocer could not possibly understand the urbane and mocking world which he inhabited on Saturday evening; and contrariwise, to enjoy the bawdy and blasphemy over coffee with these admirable friends all the more because he is aware of a "deeper," "spiritual" world within him which they cannot understand. You see the idea—the worldly friends touch him on one side and the grocer on the other, and he is the complete, balanced, complex man who sees round them all. *Thus, while being permanently treacherous to at least two sets of people, he will feel, instead of shame, a continual undercurrent of self-satisfaction.*[4]

So what are we to do in such situations? We run into them in one way or another all the time—at work, on teams, committees, with various friends and acquaintances—where we have to interact peaceably with people who hold very different worldviews than our own.

Most of us realize that we have to pick our battles; we can't directly confront each and every misstatement that comes out of someone's mouth. But is the patient's course of action here the only alternative?

For my part, if we simply and authentically be ourselves, we will make much more headway in evangelization. And at the same time, we'll be much more comfortable in our own skin—making our friendships more and more real and less superficial. What do I mean?

Let's say we just went to a weekend conference on Christ-like leadership and found it really moving; when our coworker asks Monday morning how our weekend went, our response shouldn't just be, "It was good. How was yours?" We could simply mention the conference and how moving it was; this need not be elaborate—we could do it in a single sentence by just saying something like, "It was great—I attended a conference on Christian leadership and found it really moving and inspiring." If the coworker asks

4. Ibid., 52, emphasis added.

more about the conference, then we can fill in details; if not, then we can just leave it there. But notice: this is a non-confrontational way of simply being ourselves.

Or, let's say a Catholic just had a really moving experience of Christ's mercy in the sacrament of confession. When asked about his day, he or she might say, "You know I've been a bit down lately, but I just had a wonderful experience in the sacrament of confession. Thanks for asking!"

Or, finally, here's a way that I failed to live this out recently: Shortly after Father's Day, I was going for a jog and a neighbor stopped to say hello; she then asked how my Father's Day went. I gave the ho-hum reply, "It was great—how did it go for you all?" In reality, my family and I went to see a softball game played between the priests of the Archdiocese of Kansas City, Kansas, and the priests of Kansas City, Missouri. The game was played on a professional field, using the Jumbotron and even instant replay! It was a really neat experience for my family. But in the moment, I assumed (for whatever reason) that my neighbor wouldn't be interested in such spiritual and Catholic stuff, so I kept a lid on it. In that moment, I was not really myself—and thus stifled a small opportunity for evangelization (not to mention authentic friendship).

For my part, the best way to pass on our faith is (1) to have a living faith ourselves and (2) to find ways to make this living faith known to others. This need not be in an "in your face" sort of way—all we have to do is authentically and joyfully be ourselves.

If at the work place we're perceived as a wonderful, friendly, hard-working, and honest colleague—and if, further, people notice in us a certain stability and peace—they are *not* going to just assume that the source of that character and peace is a living and personal relationship with Jesus Christ. They won't assume it unless we've made it known in some way.

By simply being ourselves, we are slowly and authentically revealing the truth about who we are and what we take life to be about. And we can do it in small, non-condemning and non-confrontational ways.

Evangelization doesn't happen overnight, but by being ourselves over the long haul, we communicate the joy and love of the gospel. And since no one can argue with our experience and our personal encounter with Christ, this shouldn't be threatening to anyone.

In fact, many such encounters over a period of time usually elicit further questions about the Christian faith and our experience with Christ. This opens the door to *welcome* dialogue; that is, it gives us an opportunity to witness to our transforming encounter with Christ and to offer Christian explanations and responses *when the hearer is disposed to listen.* When the other person is asking questions, we have a much more hospitable and friendly environment for discussion than if we were to simply take the lead and announce the Gospel unprovoked.

Lastly, look at the friendship that could blossom here. When two very different people become sincere friends, it is because both were honest and "real" with one another—and came to respect and admire each other, despite their differences. Such was certainly the case with the moving accounts of the friendship between Supreme Court Justices Antonin Scalia and Ruth Bader Ginsburg. Different as they were, they were able to be real and honest with one another, and came to esteem and respect each other tremendously, despite their obvious political differences.

But with the patient above, he is not being real with his secular friends; and the longer he is fake with them, the harder it will be for him to ever be himself. And to the extent that he is not himself—if he is not comfortable in his own skin around them—a sincere friendship cannot really develop.

But conversely, if one is real and honest (not necessarily confrontational, but just real), then a few things will result: (1) we may spread the joy of knowing Christ; (2) we will grow increasingly comfortable in our own skin, even though our friend or colleague thinks very differently than we do; and (3) we will be cultivating an authentic friendship—by being true to ourselves and having a real and honest person-to-person encounter.

So, we have nothing to lose and much to gain by simply being ourselves. People are generally fake in such situations because they want to avoid conflict. But there's a way of being ourselves *and* avoiding unnecessary conflict: simply by acknowledging our experience with Christ—which is not, of itself, subject to the truth or falsity of argument. No one can argue with our experience—it is not true or false, it is simply *our* experience. And while our experience rests upon real truth claims—the truth claims of Jesus Christ historically and his real presence in our lives today—very often, especially in our culture, people come to embrace those truth claims only *after* they have seen their existential impact in someone's life.

In order to see how we can more practically implement this in our lives—evangelizing by simply being ourselves—we will now turn to a summary of Sherry Weddell's book, *Forming Intentional Disciples*, where she delineates five distinct stages or thresholds that one typically passes through on their path to conversion. Our discussion of Weddell's book will take a few pages where we won't be referring to Screwtape. Nonetheless, this is worth our while because Weddell provides us with a clear plan of attack—a plan that would have greatly altered the way in which the patient interacted above with his friends.

Weddell's five thresholds show us that evangelization doesn't take place overnight; in fact, they strongly suggest what we have implied above—namely, that evangelization generally takes place within the context of a real and honest friendship. Further, with Weddell's model in mind, we can approach evangelization with more modest goals, which makes it less intimidating and puts less pressure on ourselves—in which case, we'll probably evangelize a lot more than we currently do.

In other words, what if we thought of our task as simply trying to accompany someone from one threshold to the next? What if, instead of trying to make someone a devout Christian overnight, we simply tried to help them move one level up? And what if I told you that all we needed to do was simply and authentically and joyfully be ourselves?

Weddell's Five Thresholds of Conversion

Trust

The first threshold is "trust," by which Weddell means some positive association with Christ or Christianity; that is, for a person to even consider converting, a bridge of trust must first exist. This "trust," or "positive association," could simply be the one Christian friend an atheist has, or some positive memory from the past of a Christian school or Christian family upbringing.[5]

If the person doesn't have this trust or positive association with Christ or anything Christian, then our job is simply to plant seeds and foster that trust; if one already has this level of positive association, then our job is to broaden and deepen that trust.[6]

Weddell notes a couple of pitfalls for the evangelist at this stage: first and foremost, we need to resist the temptation to be defensive when faced with distrust. That is, when faced with a person's negative views of Christianity, we are likely to perceive this as an attack on ourselves; but this defensiveness is counterproductive, as Weddell writes: "We need to avoid such things as defensiveness, seeing ourselves as a 'victim', and avoiding or judging those who don't trust us."[7]

An axiom I tell my students when it comes to evangelization is that *the issue is not the issue*. In other words, despite what the person says they are upset about or whatever ostensible reasons they give for their negative take on Christianity, we have to realize that the real issues often go much deeper; what the non-believer says verbally is often only scratching the surface. For this reason, before we engage, we have to try to get to the root of where the person really is spiritually. We can't get worked up over surface objections; we have to be patient—and provide a safe environment for the person to get to the real issues which are keeping them from Christ. Only when we do that will we make any substantial

---

5. Weddell, *Forming Intentional Disciples*, 132–33.

6. Ibid., 135.

7. Ibid., 133.

progress. All the doctrinal discussion in the world won't make headway if we don't get to these deeper layers.

In fact, one of Weddell's maxims is *never accept a label without a story*.[8] That is, if someone self-describes as an "atheist," don't be afraid to follow up with, "Tell me about the God you don't believe in," or simply ask, "Have you ever believed in God?" In other words, we shouldn't let someone's self-described label make us back away in a tepid manner; there's always a story that goes with the label—and very often, the story is *much* more informative than the label.[9] We will discuss this issue further when we take up the "threshold conversation" below. For now, at this stage of trust, it's often most productive simply to let the person talk and explain their spiritual journey; our job here is to listen attentively, lovingly, and non-defensively. As we said above, we are *accompanying* them on a journey.

Curiosity

Once the person has a positive association with something related to Christianity, the next stage is "curiosity." At this threshold, the person is simply "intrigued" by the person of Jesus Christ or Christianity—but is not yet really open to changing his or her life.[10] They have trust—a bridge to Christianity—and now they are curious, somewhat intrigued, as it were.

Here, Weddell advises us to tread carefully. That is, when a friend or colleague begins to show some interest, we often get excited, and we want to tell them all that we know about the Christian faith and the life of discipleship. So, another dictum I have proposed to my evangelization students is: *always assume you'll get another chance*. This may seem counterintuitive, but what often happens is that—since we fear we won't get another chance to talk openly about our faith with this particular person—we rush

8. Ibid., 129, 194.

9. See ibid., 193–94.

10. Ibid., 129.

to make sure we say everything we've been wanting to say for the past several months or even years! As one can imagine, this type of situation rarely goes well, since we end up bombarding the person with everything we've been wanting to share for months on end.

But if we assume, in the midst of the conversation, that there will be another opportunity, then we curb our inclination to vomit all of our faith knowledge on their lap in one sitting. Very often in these situations, *less is more*; and if we overwhelm them at this precious moment, we may set them back. Weddell describes well the delicacy of this stage:

> It is very important that we tread lightly here. You can easily quench inquiries by drowning a teaspoon full of curiosity with a gallon of answers. Match your response to your friend's level of curiosity, and then wait for her to become curious again.[11]

If we look at Jesus, he often answered questions *with further questions*. If anybody could've gone on for days about the mystery of God, certainly it's Jesus! But he didn't do that; he gave people what they could handle in the moment—and in doing so, he made the conversation about *them*.[12] In other words, the evangelist has to avoid the temptation to worry about how he or she looks in the conversation—the vanity of appearing to "really know one's stuff," or the appearance of "having it all together."

At the curiosity stage, we want to nourish their curiosity and give an account of our experience with Christ; but we must be leery of overestimating their interest: even if the conversation comes up, their curiosity and interest may still be very fragile and therefore needs to be handled with care.

---

11. Ibid., 145.
12. Ibid., 145–47.

Openness

The threshold of openness goes beyond curiosity in that one is now *open* to the possibility of personal and spiritual change.[13] Here, the person is sensing the possibility of real and dramatic change, but perhaps they feel they're not ready yet. In Weddell's view, this is the hardest stage for a person in our context to pass through; at this point the person is "open," but they find it very difficult to actively commit.[14]

Here, we must try to put ourselves in the other's shoes: this stage is often incredibly frightening for the one going through it, since so much of the person's world could quickly change (e.g., lifestyle, friends, habits of sex, drunkenness, drugs, pornography, etc.). We need to be sensitive to how difficult passing through this stage really is—something which long-practicing Christians often forget. If we are going to effectively and lovingly accompany someone through this stage, we must use our imagination to take ourselves back in time, remembering what it was like for us then.[15]

Seeking

The stage of seeking goes beyond openness in that one has entered a new *active* phase: the person is actively seeking answers and a spiritual home.[16] Weddell describes previous stages as essentially "passive," as one moves from a somewhat indifferent trust (first stage), to the intrigue of curiosity (second stage), and then to the consideration of a personal and spiritual reorientation of one's life (third stage).[17]

When one has entered the threshold of seeking, one is now especially ready and open to catechesis and Christian teaching.[18]

---

13. Ibid., 156.
14. Ibid.
15. Ibid., 156–57.
16. Ibid., 171–73.
17. Ibid., 171.
18. Ibid., 176.

That is, before this point, the evangelist needs to tend first to the heart—seeking to massage the heart and till the soil of one's soul in preparation for the engagement of the mind. In earlier stages, apologetics and catechesis are often not received well because the heart of the hearer is not yet open.[19] In fact, in our context, *the path to the head often lies through the heart*. But now, in the "seeking" stage, we have an ideal setting for Christian intellectual formation.

Becoming an Intentional Disciple

The final threshold is becoming an "intentional disciple," by which Weddell means that one has made a conscious commitment to follow Jesus Christ in a personal and living way. At this point, one has made an intentional decision to follow Christ; one is no longer a Christian because their parents were, or because all of their friends are. At this point, one has said "yes" to Christ's marriage proposal and seeks to live this out in a deliberate and intentional way.

When someone is on the cusp of entering the threshold of becoming an intentional disciple, Weddell recommends actually proposing this to the person, asking them if they are ready to make a conscious commitment. If someone says "no," Weddell suggests asking what the reason is, in order to find out what is holding them back.[20]

As one can see, for Weddell, the goal of evangelization is not only to help someone *become* a Christian, but to help them *mature* as a Christian and grow daily as an *intentional* disciple; in this sense, conversion is always ongoing.

What makes Weddell's model so helpful is that having a sense for the various thresholds empowers us to view evangelization as simply befriending people and accompanying them from one threshold to another. As I suggested above, the all-or-nothing categories in which we often operate put tremendous pressure on us and often keep us from evangelizing. But if we approach

19. Ibid., 126.
20. Ibid., 179.

evangelization with more modest goals—thinking in terms of thresholds—we can approach evangelization through the context of friendship. If we are accompanying people on their journey in a loving way, from one threshold to the next, then all we have to do is joyfully be ourselves.

Next, we discuss the "threshold conversation" and the absolute centrality of a personal relationship with God—both for ourselves and for evangelization.

Threshold Conversation

In order to facilitate a person's movement from one threshold to another, Weddell proposes the "threshold conversation," which is basically where we inquire about a person's lived relationship with God. Here, we're trying to get the person to open up about their *lived* relationship (or lack thereof) with God.[21]

For Weddell, again, this is not the time to correct all their misstatements or even to offer our own testimony, but simply to listen lovingly and attentively—both to the details *and* to the emotional content of their story.[22] We also want to assess which threshold they are in, and then try to accompany and assist them on their journey to the next one.

Weddell rightly points out that no one can move beyond the stage of curiosity unless they are convinced that a *personal* relationship with God is possible.[23] Surprisingly, many long self-professed Christians subtly walk around with a deistic view of God—that is, a view that sees God as the uncaused Cause of the universe, but who does not actively interact with his creation in prayer and the like. Perhaps they believe this God even sent his Son long ago, but they often don't truly believe they can encounter him in the present in a living, real, and personal way. The threshold conversation helps to bring this to light and provides an occasion to encourage

21. Ibid., 191–93.
22. Ibid., 193.
23. Ibid., 144.

the person to take the "dare" of encountering the living God in this personal way.

Further, when we invite someone to open up about their lived relationship with God (or lack thereof), we're giving them one of the few opportunities they may have to discuss God openly and the possibility of having a relationship with him. If we never bring up this possibility, most people aren't going to just pursue it themselves. Many people don't know—or don't believe—that such a relationship is even possible. And if we don't talk about it, this isn't going to change any time soon. In fact, our silence only reinforces their doubt.

For Weddell, spinning our wheels discussing doctrine won't be evangelically fruitful if we neglect the absolute centrality of this personal relationship with God. In other words, we have to cut through the ostensible reasons and objections given for not being a Christian and get to the very heart of the matter—namely, *this living relationship*. The doctrine is important—even essential—but it must be contextualized by this living relationship of love.

As we have said, the threshold conversation is not the time to address all of their "incorrect" beliefs; for Weddell, allowing someone to discuss their unbelief openly tends *not* to reinforce their unbelief—in fact, sometimes it can be therapeutic in moving them closer to belief.[24]

Further, the person "going off" on their unbelief will often be surprised by our gentleness and willingness to simply listen—to listen without having all the answers ready at hand. Such listening is essential for our future proclamation of the gospel. For here as elsewhere in life, we must earn the right to be heard—and we do this by listening first with love. As Weddell writes, "We will never evangelize what we do not love."[25]

24. Ibid., 197.
25. Ibid., 136.

Another Motive

As a motive for evangelization—beyond simply heaven and hell (which, of course, should be more than enough!)—let us think back to our own lives before we committed consciously and intentionally to a life of Christian discipleship: what did our interior lives look like—especially our psychological and emotional lives? For many of us, before we really "knew" Christ and walked with him daily, our lives were filled with anxieties and insecurities, struggling to find self-worth in a performance-driven world—measuring ourselves by trying to climb social ladders or meeting up to secular standards of "success" (sports, academics, looks, physique, etc.).

For many of us, our interior lives were in disarray before we knew Christ, and our emotional demeanor went up and down with how these things were going on the outside. But after knowing Christ in a deep and personal way, many of us have found a deeper and abiding stability and peace—a peace that the world cannot give.[26]

So the question is this: do we want other people to experience the same joy and peace of knowing Christ that we have found? When we think back to where we were *before* we knew Christ, most of us would never want to go back. So, if we truly love people, this thought alone should move us to evangelize—to share with others what we have so joyously found and have come to treasure, both in this life and the next.

It's not just about saving people from hell; it's also about saving them from the "hell" of the present—the hell of a life riddled with anxiety, always trying to "make it" and trying to "look the part," and never feeling like one is enough—something certainly exacerbated in age of social media, where our lives are on constant display for all to judge and compare.[27]

26. My own conversion story can be found in my book *John Paul II to Aristotle and Back Again*, 49–53.

27. My wife captures this in her book with the phrase "the world's idea of perfect"—which seems to have such a hold over us, pressuring us constantly to look and be the part. See Sarah Swafford, *Emotional Virtue*, 17–24.

Christ has saved us from sin and death, but he also wishes to redeem us from the peculiar sorrow, loneliness, insecurity, and anxiety of our current age.

We are the pearl of great price in God's eyes—the one lamb sought by the shepherd who left the ninety-nine! But we don't see or feel our worth until we really know and encounter the love of Christ. There's nothing the secular world can offer that can match the unshakable peace and joy of knowing Christ. And if we really love others, won't we want to share this with them?

In the next chapter we shift gears a bit, discussing—of all things—*laughter*. Once again, Screwtape sees so much more in the little things than we do; as we saw in the first chapter, he wants to *divide*, and he will use whatever is at his disposal to do so—even laughter. At the same time, Screwtape is quick to recognize that some laughter *unites*, in which case it works directly against his purposes.

So, to the various causes of laughter, and how Screwtape sees them working for or against his cause, we now turn.

Chapter 4

Letter 11: Joy and Sarcasm

IN LETTER 11, SCREWTAPE discusses the causes of human laughter and how each type either favors his work, or that of the Enemy (i.e., God); he names four causes: joy, fun, the joke proper, and flippancy. What we find is that some of these bring people together, while others tear people apart—and Screwtape certainly favors the latter.

Joy

Screwtape sees laughter caused by joy as decidedly *not* on his side because it's ultimately the fruit of affection between people—both as a bonding force and as the fruit of that bond.

As I joke with my male students, "How do you know if a certain lady friend has interest in you? *If she laughs at your jokes!*" Here, the cause of laughter is not so much the joke itself (as we know all too well!), but rather (and primarily) the affection between the budding couple. In this same vein, Screwtape writes:

> You see the first [laughter caused by joy] among friends and lovers reunited on the eve of a holiday. Among adults some pretext in the way of jokes is usually provided, *but the facility with which the smallest witticisms produce laughter at such a time shows that they are not the real cause.*[1]

As is obviously the case, laughter caused by joy flows from affection and love—and for that reason, Screwtape despises it and sees it as working diametrically against his aims.

1. Lewis, *Screwtape Letters*, 53, emphasis added.

Fun

The second cause of laughter is fun. Now at first glance, one might assume that surely "fun" favors the work of Screwtape—since it takes us away from more "important" matters of religious duty and devotion. And Screwtape does acknowledge this potential: "It can sometimes be used . . . to divert humans from something else which the Enemy [God] would like them to be feeling or doing."[2]

But because fun also produces affection between people, Screwtape asserts that "it is of very little use to us."[3] In fact, he goes on to say that it "promotes charity, courage, contentment, and many other evils."[4]

In his demonic designs, Screwtape wants division, isolation, loneliness, and despair. For that reason, laughter caused by "fun" is ultimately on the side of the Enemy (i.e., God), despite its occasional advantage of encouraging diversion and distraction.

The Joke Proper

Screwtape here alludes to the long-standing philosophical tradition that sees risibility—the ability to laugh—as something flowing from our rationality. This is seen, for example, in the double meaning that accompanies many jokes—where the humor is taken precisely from the fact that a word can be taken in two distinct ways. And so Screwtape writes, "The Joke Proper . . . turns on sudden perception of *incongruity*."[5]

To give one example, my wife and I (and our kids) were once on a long road trip, and through the wonderful experience of a long car ride, my wife eventually blurted out: "I'm starting to lose my *patience*." To which someone in the back replied: "*Good thing you're not a doctor!*"

2. Ibid., 54.
3. Ibid.
4. Ibid.
5. Iibid., emphasis added.

Or, one of my favorite commercials is the one from Buffalo Wild Wings which first shows two guys at the restaurant watching a game. The one guy tells the other that he can stay longer because he left a note for his wife. The next scene shows the wife and kids at home in the kitchen with a police officer, with the officer holding up the note, which reads: "We have your husband, don't call the police." The officer then turns to the distressed wife and says: "This doesn't look good." As the wife gasps, the officer continues: "*A bunch of different fonts, couple of typos.*"

The joke, of course, is that the wife takes the officer's comment ("This doesn't look good") as referring to her husband's safety and well-being, but the officer actually meant it as an evaluation of the *aesthetic* quality of the note (and in the commercial itself, one can see the note with all the differently sized letters and colors—something a kindergartener might have put together!).

What makes the commercial funny is the rational play between the two different meanings of "This doesn't look good." This is a distinctly human capacity. While animals certainly can communicate, one will not find any time soon, say, a dog making a pun on words and utilizing double meaning to elicit laughter. In this sense, jokes are eminently *human* and should be cultivated as something positively good—as an expression of our rational nature. They are part of a full human life.

So how might the joke work in Screwtape's favor—perhaps by resorting to vulgarity? While Screwtape does acknowledge this possibility, he makes it quite clear that his principal use lies elsewhere.

For Screwtape, the real use of jokes lay in their *all-excusing* nature. In other words, if something can be passed off as a joke, many otherwise less-than-noble actions can get a pass: "Hence it is invaluable as a means of destroying shame."[6] For Screwtape, this all-excusing nature of humor is far more valuable than simple vulgarity:

> A thousand bawdy or even blasphemous jokes do not
> help toward a man's damnation so much as the discovery
> that almost anything he wants to do can be done, *not only*

6. Ibid., 55.

*without the disapproval but with the admiration of his fel-
lows*, if only it can get itself treated as a Joke.[7]

Screwtape offers examples of being cheap, cowardice, and
cruelty—all of which would ordinarily be frowned upon—that is,
"*unless the cruel man can represent it as a practical joke.*"[8] If the
man boasts of letting others pay for him in a joking manner, he
becomes not cheap but a "comical fellow." And: "Mere cowardice is
shameful; cowardice boasted of with humorous exaggerations and
grotesque gestures can be passed off as funny."[9]

In this manner, vice gets a pass, precisely because it's "funny."
And what's funny need not be held accountable and need not be
challenged; in fact, it may well be applauded.

Flippancy

But flippancy, for Screwtape, is the "best of all."[10] Flippancy here is
somewhat hard to define, but we all know it when we see it—and
we've all seen it before. It represents a sort of cynical and sarcastic
attitude that subtly undermines something good. For Screwtape,
not much of a joke is really even told: "Only a clever human can
make a real joke about virtue, or indeed about anything else; *any of
them can be trained to talk as if virtue were funny.*"[11]

Notice here how the good has become the object of derision
and laughter. Flippancy subtly suggests that something good (here
for example, virtue) is silly and need not be taken seriously—in
which case one doesn't need to worry about failing to live up to
it. In this sense, flippancy is a self-inoculation of sorts against the
demands of pursuing real human excellence.

One sees this readily with chastity: if I make fun of chastity
and present it as ridiculous, then I do not have to take its challenge

---

7. Ibid., 55–56, emphasis added.
8. Ibid., 55, emphasis added.
9. Ibid.
10. Ibid., 56.
11. Ibid., emphasis added.

to heart; I do not have to feel bad about failing to live up to it. By putting others down who do respond to this challenge, I can feel better about myself for not doing so. Screwtape writes:

> Among flippant people the joke is always assumed to have been made. No one actually makes it; *but every serious subject is discussed in a manner which implies that they have already found a ridiculous side to it.*[12]

As we have seen, Screwtape sees the task of leading some-one to damnation as one that is very subtle—taking advantage of habits that might at first seem like no big deal. Flippancy here is not a certain kind of joke; it's more of an attitude—a demeanor. And once it becomes entrenched, Screwtape sees it as the finest of armor for keeping one away from God:

> If prolonged, the habit of flippancy builds up around a man the finest armor-plaiting against the Enemy [God] that I know, and it is quite free from the dangers inherent in the other sources of laughter. It is a thousand miles away from joy; it deadens, instead of sharpening, the intellect; and it excites no affection between those who practice it.[13]

Sarcasm

While Screwtape does not directly bring up sarcasm in this letter, it readily fits in with our discussion. Obviously, there is a place for sarcasm when people know each other well. But there can be a latent danger here that can significantly undermine relationships and the affection between people.

One can readily imagine a situation where one person levels a sarcastic comment against another; and let's say this comment, while presented as a joke, clearly bears underneath it a sense of what one *really* thinks. Such a sarcastic comment becomes a clear "jab" at

12. Ibid., emphasis added.

13. Ibid.

the other—a verbal attack. But when the other person gets upset, the response is simply: "Hey, man, I was just joking—lighten up."

Here, sarcasm becomes a verbal put-down that is literally unassailable: presented under the guise of a joke, the person doesn't have to stand by the comment and defend it in a potentially confrontational manner; thus, it becomes a *cowardly* verbal attack against the other. Rather than engaging the person directly, sarcasm can be a cover to say what one wants to say but does not have the guts to say directly.

This pattern erodes communion between people; there is no real communication going on and thus no real conflict resolution. All that happens are jabs and hurt—and an inability for the hurt person to respond in a constructive manner, leaving them hurt *and* resentful. Such a pattern destroys joy and affection and leads to heartache and bitterness.

As I said, there certainly can be a place for sarcastic humor, especially when people know each other well. But the pattern above is all too easy to fall into—especially among people who share close quarters, e.g., siblings, roommates, or even spouses. We must be careful not to use humor as a weak and cowardly way to hurt the other person since, as we have said, there is no real way for the other person to respond effectively. It is in the truest sense of the phrase *not* a "fair fight," which is precisely why it leads to such corrosive and bitter resentment.

In the next chapter, we continue discussing the gradual ways in which Screwtape seeks to bring about our destruction—in fact, here he tells us directly that the most efficient and sure path to hell is the *gradual* one. And keeping us from intimate prayer with our Lord is his most steady and sure way to make this happen.

Chapter 5

Letter 12: The Safest Road to Hell

IN LETTER 12, SCREWTAPE insists that the patient must never be made aware of his true position; that is, the subtle ways in which Screwtape and Wormwood have sought to influence him and move him away from Christ must be kept from the clear view of his consciousness.

Screwtape wants the man to see these changes (e.g., his new friends) as "trivial and revocable,"[1] as if they could be easily taken back whenever he would like. In this way, the patient is slowly lulled to sleep, though he remains dimly aware that something is not quite right.

Dim Uneasiness

What Screwtape wants more than anything is for the patient to live in this state of "dim uneasiness." He does not want this uneasiness to become too strong—for if it did, it might lead to repentance and contrition, thereby bringing the patient back to the Enemy (God). Nonetheless, Screwtape does want to maintain *some* uneasiness in the patient—a *dim* uneasiness is the perfect recipe: this slight uneasiness keeps the patient from really wanting to encounter God in the present. Screwtape explains:

> This dim uneasiness needs careful handling. If it gets too strong it may wake him up and spoil the whole game. . . . If such a feeling is allowed to live, but not allowed to become irresistible and flower into real repentance, it has

1. Lewis, *Screwtape Letters*, 57.

one invaluable tendency. *It increases the patient's reluctance to think about the Enemy.*[2]

So Screwtape wants the patient to feel some uneasiness, but not too much; for too much could backfire and lead the patient directly back to the Enemy. But a little uneasiness—especially if the patient blithely sees it as no big deal—is exactly what Screwtape wants. Let's go further in understanding why this is so.

Serious Sin and Mental Prayer

In a state of uneasiness—where we know we have taken steps (however small) away from God—we really do not want direct contact with God; in such a situation *silence is loud*, even deafening—and we can't handle it. We don't want to face our thoughts; we don't *really* want to hear God's voice, because deep down we already know what we're going to hear and we're not ready for it at the moment.

It's been said that one cannot persevere in "mental prayer"— the type of prayer where we really *listen* to the voice of God—*and* serious sin: *either* we will stop praying, *or* we will stop sinning. Only for a while can we persist in both—eventually one will give way to the other.

By mental prayer, we mean quiet time with the Lord: that time where we seek to reestablish the rhythm of our lives—our thoughts, desires, and aspirations—and align them with the promptings of the Holy Spirit. On the one hand, one *can* offer all kinds of vocal prayer and even participate in praising God communally—and yet live a totally separate life of sin, and this can go on for quite some time. But on the other hand, when we stop and listen—when we really converse with the living God—it's very hard not to hear his knock on our hearts; and the more persistent we are with this type of prayer, the louder that knock gets each and every day.

It doesn't have to be a long time, but ten to twenty minutes each day of quiet conversation and listening to the Lord will

2. Ibid., 58, emphasis added.

dramatically change one's life. It might begin with reading Scripture, but it has to be a different kind of reading—it has to be one where the words come alive in the present. It has to be slow; and eventually one has to leave the text and ask the Holy Spirit for guidance in discerning what the living God is saying to us *right now*.

If one perseveres in this type of prayer, eventually one's whole life begins to change; Christ's mind and heart becomes our mind and heart. By no means does this mean moral perfection, but it does mean a heart that seeks to encounter the living God and to be in tune with the Father's will from the inside out—not out of duty, but out of love.

Screwtape realizes that the "dim uneasiness" of which he speaks is a surefire way to thwart such heartfelt prayer: when we know some things in our life have changed for the worse—that we have moved away from God in subtle and gradual ways—the last thing we want to do is spend quiet time with him in prayer. Again, we may still attend worship services—and these are in fact essential to our lives. But to make those worship services and liturgies really come alive, we need to spend some quiet moments with the Lord and listen to his call for our lives in a *personal* and living way.

As an analogy, in marriage the sexual act is in a real way the objective height of intimacy and consummation of the marital bond. But it would be a strange marriage indeed if a couple simply consummated the marital act and didn't spend time together in quiet conversation. In a similar way, receiving communion on Sunday is something like our marital consummation with God—or, we might say that earthly marital consummation points to this even greater spousal union with God.

But as with marriage, those quiet moments of personal conversation with God prepare for and make fruitful our liturgical consummation. Here we see the need for *both* private and communal prayer; Screwtape knows how essential the former is and that's why he seeks to cultivate this "dim uneasiness" in the patient, as a way to prevent it. For Screwtape, preventing such intimate prayer is invaluable for keeping us out of the Enemy's camp.

Sloth, Boredom, and Restlessness

Further, the patient is moving in the spiritual domain of sloth. While many people think of sloth as simply laziness, it's certainly more nuanced than that. Sloth can be identified as *spiritual* laziness—a state of lethargy and indifference about the highest things. But notice: many people can be in a state of sloth *and* still live a life of hyper-busyness and activity; many become workaholics for this very reason—to drown out the ache they feel on account of being spiritually unfulfilled in a deep and abiding way. In this sense, what may look like hard work on the outside may in fact be the fruit of spiritual sloth on the inside.[3]

Many others in this state of spiritual restlessness seek constant entertainment. And in our culture, screens abound in one way or another—whether it's television, video games, YouTube videos, or some other form of social media. How many of us have wasted countless and precious hours surfing the Internet or moving from one screen to the next?

Not that these things are inherently evil by any means, but their prolonged use can be symptomatic of a deep spiritual sadness and restlessness. It is in this sense that the thirteenth-century philosopher and theologian St. Thomas Aquinas defined sloth as "sorrow at the difficulty of a spiritual good."[4] We want to be great, but greatness seems too far out of reach; and so we just find other distractions to pass the time—and become sad, bored, and restless in the process.

If we are made for more and we fill ourselves with less, we shouldn't be surprised to find ourselves empty inside. We shouldn't be surprised to find ourselves bored and restless with life; and we shouldn't be surprised to find ourselves turning to work, social status, or entertainment—either to be the "gods" we chase after, or the "aspirin" that dulls our lack of purpose and meaning in life.

---

3. For more on sloth, see my *John Paul II to Aristotle and Back Again*, 43. See also Nault, *Noonday Devil*, 30–36, and Snell, *Acedia and Its Discontents*, 59–70.

4. Aquinas, *Summa Theologica*, II-IIae, q. 35., a. 1.

Screwtape sees this trajectory in exactly the same way: this "dim uneasiness" keeps the patient from encountering the living God *and* it brings him to a state of sloth—a state of boredom, meaninglessness, and hopelessness. Screwtape writes:

> You no longer need a good book which he really likes to keep him from his prayers or work or his sleep; a column of advertisements in yesterday's paper will do. You can make him waste his time not only in conversation he enjoys with people whom he likes, but in conversations with those he cares nothing about on subjects that bore him. You can make him do nothing at all for long periods. You can keep him up late at night . . . staring at a dead fire in a cold room.[5]

So the "game" for Screwtape is to get the patient away from God *and* have him lose himself in the process. In the next chapter, we will talk more about the different ways in which both God and Screwtape want the patient to "lose" himself. For now, let us note that Screwtape wants the patient to abandon his true self—his deepest and most authentic desires—in favor of a dull existence where his time is wasted in boredom, restlessness, and ultimately sadness. All of this comes to a head in one of the most heart-wrenching of Screwtape's statements:

> All the healthy and out-going activities which we want him to avoid can be inhibited and *nothing* given in return, so that at last he may say, as one of my own patients said on his arrival down here [i.e., to hell], "I now see that I spent most of my life doing *neither* I what ought, *nor* what I like."[6]

---

5. Lewis, *Screwtape Letters*, 59–60.

6. Ibid., 60, emphasis original. Screwtape continues here, stating: "The Christians describe the Enemy as one 'without whom Nothing is strong.' And Nothing is very strong: strong enough to steal away a man's best years not in sweet sins but in a dreary flickering of the mind over it knows not what and knows not why, in the gratification of curiosities so feeble that the man is only half aware of them, drumming of fingers and kicking of heels, in whistling tunes that he does not like, or in the long, dim labyrinth of reveries that have not even lust or ambition to give them a relish, but which, once chance association has started them, the

The Gradual Road

Screwtape often chides his nephew demon, Wormwood, for being too infatuated with big and exciting sins; for Screwtape, it doesn't matter *what* the sin is—as long as it leads the person away from God. And he would happily resort to the mundane, which for the most part bypasses our consciousness and lulls us to sleep. Indeed, the gradual and subtle road, as we've seen throughout, can be deadly if we're not careful. Screwtape especially knows this to be true and he seeks at every moment to exploit this against the patient:

> Murder is no better than cards if cards can do the trick. Indeed *the safest road to Hell is the gradual one*—the gentle slope, soft underfoot, without sudden turnings, *without milestones, without signposts.*[7]

For our purposes, while this is a wake-up call, it's not a call to despair. It is a call to "enjoy the ride"—to realize the momentous importance of life and live it to the full *right now*. Right now—not after "this thing gets done," or after "this stressful situation is over with," or "after I finish school and get a job." The time to encounter "real" life and the living God is *now*.

The ploy of the devil is to trap us in worry, anxiety, and insecurity—and then lead us to outlets that waste away the precious years of our life, so that our lives will be spent doing "neither what I ought, nor what I liked," as Screwtape said above.

Occasionally, some of my students have taken C. S. Lewis's *Screwtape Letters* in a somewhat despairing way. For most others, it has opened their eyes to the paramount importance of the little things—and that insight has given them great hope and confidence and a renewed sense of purpose for every facet of their life. My hope is that the latter will be your response as well; we have nothing to fear—*except* not really living. But if our eyes are open and we are attuned to the importance of the little things, we will make

---

creature is too weak and fuddled to shake off" (ibid.).

7. Ibid., 61, emphasis added.

ourselves immune to Screwtape's attacks—and probably enjoy life a whole lot more in the process.

In the next chapter, we explore more fully how God wants us to be our true selves—indeed, the very best version of ourselves. As mentioned above, there is a sense in which both God and Screwtape want us to abandon ourselves; but the paradox is that in abandoning ourselves to God, we become more fully ourselves than ever before.

Conversely, as we've begun to see in this chapter, Screwtape wants us to abandon our true selves as a means—not only to separate us eternally from God, but also to bring us to a sad and unfulfilled state. Indeed, Screwtape wants us to be happy neither in this life, nor the next.

Chapter 6

Letter 13: The Sadness of One's Ego

THE SCENE IN LETTER 13 is that the patient has had a second conversion of sorts and Screwtape is not happy. What interests us here is how this renewal came about and what it means for us today—especially with regard to the different ways in which both Screwtape and God want us to "lose" ourselves.

Our True Selves

Screwtape recounts two "blunders" of Wormwood that helped lead to this spiritual renewal: first, Wormwood allowed the man to read a book he really likes, simply because he likes it; and second, he allowed the patient to take a walk through the countryside, which he especially enjoys.[1]

While these seem like trivial actions in the grand scheme of things, Screwtape's recounting of the book is especially noteworthy; he sees a sort of innocent pleasure in reading a book one enjoys *precisely because one enjoys it*—and not simply to be part of the in-crowd: "On your own showing you first of all allowed the patient to read a book he really enjoyed, because he enjoyed it *and not in order to make clever remarks about it to his new friends.*"[2] Here, the vanity of the patient is being overcome by his immersing himself in something he enjoys for its own sake—and not for the sake of what others think.

---

1. Lewis, *Screwtape*, 63–64.
2. Ibid., emphasis added.

There is an innocence here that is often lost on our culture for a couple of reasons: first, we seldom take time for such leisure—we are most definitely an "on the go" culture, seemingly from the womb; and secondly, our vanity often gets the best of us, as we put pressure on ourselves to do and enjoy what everyone else is doing (e.g., social media, television shows, watching sports), since we don't want to be left out.

Losing Ourselves

Screwtape is very clear that in order to detach the patient from the Enemy (God), the patient must be detached from his deepest self.[3] The reason is because when the patient taps into his deepest desires, he is actually on the path to God, as Screwtape suggests here: "The deepest likings and impulses of any man are the raw material, the starting-point, with which the Enemy has furnished him."[4]

While God does seek to purify us—and asks us to forfeit the lesser part of ourselves—he does so in order that we may become more fully ourselves than ever before. Screwtape explains:

> Of course I know that the Enemy also wants to detach men from themselves, but in a different way. Remember always, that He really likes the little vermin, and sets an absurd value on the distinctness of every one of them. When He talks of their losing their selves, He only means abandoning the clamor of self-will; once they have done that, He really gives them back all their personality, and boasts (I am afraid, sincerely) that when they are wholly His *they will be more themselves than ever*.[5]

Many spiritual writers over the years have long noted that our deepest desires often reveal God's calling for our lives—that God has planted these desires in our hearts in order to move us toward his will.

3. Ibid., 65.
4. Ibid.
5. Ibid., emphasis added.

Initially, of course, there will be conflict between our wills and his. But once we scrape away the sin, selfishness, fear, and anxiety—once those superficial layers of ourselves have been purified—we will find our deepest desires aligning with God's will.[6] And we should have confidence that when we follow God's will, it will lead to our ultimate happiness.

On the other hand, the demonic goal is always to get us away from our true selves, in order to make us try to become something we're not:

> To get him away from those [the patient's deepest likings] is therefore always a point gained; even in things indifferent it is always desirable to substitute the standards of the World, or convention, or fashion, for a human's own real likings and dislikings. . . . I would make it a rule to eradicate from my patient any strong personal taste which is not actually a sin, even if it is something quite trivial such as fondness for county cricket or collecting stamps or drinking cocoa.[7]

Self-Absorbed or Self-Forgetful

What Screwtape detests about such personal hobbies and interests is that there is a sort of innocence and humility about them; there is a real sense in which such actions directly oppose the vanity of worrying about what everyone else thinks. And the less concerned we are with the vanity of what others think, the less preoccupied we are with ourselves. When we throw ourselves into some hobby or

6. The "lesser" part of any athlete is first at variance with his or her coach's conditioning program. But as time goes on and the athlete grows in stamina, the athlete sees the wisdom in the coach's program. And as things mature, one sees the union of the athlete's will with that of the coach. In a sense, at the beginning the coach wanted the athlete to achieve excellence *more* than the athlete did, but as the athlete "lost" his or herself in the beginning, the result turned into immense gain—the athlete has become what he or she truly wanted to be from the beginning. The same is of course true in attaining excellence in many other areas, such as music, academics, acting, dance, etc.

7. Ibid., 65–66.

activity just for the joy of it, we are losing ourselves in the reality we are engaged in. Instead of an inward "navel-gazing," we are orienting ourselves outward—to the world, to others, and ultimately to God.

As we mentioned in the first chapter, one often meets people who are entrapped in a sort of self-preoccupation; often, we wonder if they are really listening when we speak to them; they seemingly have an inability to truly enter our world. As we speak, we can tell that their minds are elsewhere—that they are consumed with something else and are not really present. We know how painful this can be, especially when it becomes a pattern.

For that reason, we need to *not* be that person ourselves. When others speak to us, do we truly enter their world? Or, are we looking over their shoulder? Are we just thinking about what we have to do later that day, or what *we* happen to be worried about?

We must first *be* the change we want to see happen. When we sincerely forget ourselves, there is a kind of dance that can happen, say, in a conversation—where we get lost in the ebb and flow of the discussion and truly enter the world of the other person.

On the other hand, when we're focused on ourselves and how we look, we're almost "watching" ourselves have the conversation as it's happening; our mind runs with thoughts like: "How did I sound just there? What are they thinking of me? Did I come across the way I wanted to?" Here, the excessive preoccupation with ourselves creates something of a stutter. We are turned inward and are unable to rise above ourselves and truly enter into the world of the other. And the paradox, of course, is that usually we come across much better when we're not worried about it.

To take a slightly different analogy, imagine a kid playing with a bug—the kid is totally lost in its fascination. He's not worried about what others think, or whether his actions will help him climb some social ladder. Indeed, there is something anti-utilitarian about what he is doing; playing with the bug is its own end; it is certainly not a means to something else.

Compare this with the pursuit of a marketing campaign aimed solely at making more profit. While sometimes we have to do certain things not for their own sake, but as a means to some other end (after all, the bills do have to be paid), still, in our modern context we hardly ever do things just for the joy of doing them; we hardly ever allow ourselves the chance to literally lose ourselves in some activity, just for the joy of it. And when we actually do take the time for such things, we generally feel more at home and at peace with ourselves; it brings us into closer contact with reality—the world as it is—and not simply the constructs of our modern world, which usually revolve around either the marketplace or our social or political positioning.

Screwtape is acutely aware of the danger to his cause when human beings are true to themselves—when they truly immerse themselves in something they enjoy for its own sake:

> Such things, I grant you, have nothing of virtue in them, *but there is a sort of innocence and humility and self-forgetfulness about them which I distrust.* The man who truly and disinterestedly enjoys any one thing in the world, for its own sake, and without caring two-pence what other people say about it, is by that very fact forearmed against some of our subtlest modes of attack. You should always try to make the patient abandon the people or food or books he really likes in favor of the "best" people, the "right" food, and the "important" books.[8]

The Sadness of One's Ego

If we live our lives and make our decisions based solely on what others think, we never become our truest and deepest selves. Life passes us by and we are only in contact with a sort of façade of reality; as we have seen, in this situation, we find ourselves far from God *and* unfulfilled. We are never enough, never happy, and often lonely. There's a joke I once came across that speaks to this that goes something like this:

> When I was twenty, I worried about what people thought of me; when I turned forty, I decided I didn't care what

---

8. Ibid., 66, emphasis added.

others thought of me; then I turned sixty, and I real-
ized—*no one was ever thinking of me!*

There's a narcissism in our culture that sometimes passes
under the guise of modesty: "I am not fully secure and confident
in myself, so I will follow the lead of what others think." But the
spiritual disease and suffering here is an overpreoccupation with
oneself. To the extent that I am constantly concerned with the ap-
proval of others, to that extent I am focused on myself. And the
more self-preoccupied I am, the less free I am to truly love and
immerse myself in the world around me.

And as I live more and more in this self-concerned and narcissistic way, I tend to become more and more unsatisfied and restless. In a strange way, one can be both narcissistic *and* sad. In fact,
they may go together more often than we realize—since when we
are down, we tend to turn inward, often only thinking about ourselves and how we feel. But on the other hand, the more we forget
ourselves and lose ourselves in the world and the people around
us, the happier we tend to be. And the more we lose ourselves in
things that really matter, the more we find God in our lives.

This is the lesson Screwtape unwittingly teaches us in this letter. In God's call for us to "lose" ourselves, paradoxically, we find
our truest and deepest self. In giving, we receive; and in making a
gift of our lives, we find ourselves enriched immeasurably. Whereas
Screwtape's call for us to lose ourselves turns us inward—making
us sad, restless, and bored.

Jesus' antidote for a culture under the anguish of anxiety and
self-centered worry ("Am I enough? Will I ever be enough?") is
simply to break out of our own ego and love our neighbor. Perhaps
even before we turn to God in prayer, our first step in breaking
these shackles that constantly turn us inward is to think less about
ourselves and love more—to be less self-concerned and more
self-forgetful.

And a small step along that road may well be to pursue the
smallest of things—not because they are popular or will position
us better socially, but just because we enjoy them. After all, as
Screwtape said above: "there is a sort of innocence and humility and

self-forgetfulness about them which I distrust."[9] These thoughts from a "demon" may well be much more insightful with regard to our own happiness and fulfillment than we could ever imagine.

In the next chapter, we will treat humility directly—which, according to Screwtape, finds its goal and purpose in the service of love: as he explains, the very purpose of humility is to take our eyes off ourselves and turn them outward in love of God and neighbor. And when we do that, perhaps paradoxically, we actually come to an even greater and deeper love of *ourselves*.

9. Ibid.

Chapter 7

Letter 14: Humility and the Accuser

BY LETTER 14, SCREWTAPE bemoans the fact that the patient has become humble.[1] Screwtape then seeks to undermine this development, chiefly through inculcating in the patient a distorted sense of humility. In the process—with his own demonic clarity—he explains very clearly why the Enemy (God) so desires this particular virtue and why it's so important. Thus, in this letter, we get a keen glimpse at the essence and purpose of humility from God's point of view—a vantage point, as we have seen throughout, that Screwtape understands surprisingly well.

Thinking Less about Ourselves

Screwtape sees the chief purpose of humility and the life of virtue as orienting ourselves outward—taking our eyes off ourselves and turning them outward in love of God and neighbor. He writes: "By this virtue [humility], as by all the others, our Enemy wants to turn the man's attention away from self, to Him and the man's neighbors."[2]

However, we often view humility as a certain low opinion of ourselves, as if humility entailed the denial and rejection of our real gifts and talents. This is exactly the way Screwtape wants us to see things:

> You [Wormwood] must therefore conceal from the patient the true end of Humility. Let him think of it not as

1. Lewis, *Screwtape Letters*, 69.
2. Ibid., 70.

self-forgetfulness but as a certain kind of opinion (namely, a low opinion) of his own talents and character.[3]

Ironically, this distortion of humility has the effect of dramatically undermining its virtuous quality; instead of "self-forgetfulness," this distorted view of humility paradoxically *turns our minds back upon ourselves*:

> By this method thousands of humans have been brought to think that humility means pretty women trying to believe they are ugly and clever men trying to believe they are fools. And since what they are trying to believe may in some cases be manifest nonsense, they cannot succeed in believing it and we have the chance of *keeping their minds endlessly revolving on themselves* in an effort to achieve the impossible.[4]

Screwtape goes on to give telling examples of true humility (from God's point of view), explaining how humility frees us to love others *and* ourselves:

> The Enemy wants to bring the man to a state of mind in which he could design the best cathedral in the world and know it to be the best and rejoice in the fact, without being any more (or less) or otherwise glad at having done it than he would be if it had been done by another. The Enemy wants him, in the end, to be so free from any bias in his own favor that he can rejoice in his own talents as frankly and gratefully as in his neighbor's talents—or in a sunrise, an elephant, or a waterfall. He wants each man, in the long run, to be able to recognize all creatures (even himself) as glorious and excellent things. He wants to kill their animal self-love as soon as possible; but it is His long-term policy, I fear, to restore to them a new kind of self-love—charity and gratitude for all selves, including their own; *when they have really learned to love their neighbors as themselves, they will be allowed to love themselves as their neighbors.* . . . He would rather the man thought himself a great architect or a great poet and then

3. Ibid.
4. Ibid., 70–71, emphasis added.

forgot about it, than that he should spend much time and pains trying to think himself a bad one.[5]

Even of Our Sins

This view of humility as the virtue that makes love possible—by turning us outward and taking our attention off ourselves—makes sense with respect to our gifts, talents, and accomplishments; but what about our *weaknesses*? Is it possible to be narcissistic by being *overly concerned with our faults and limitations*?

That's exactly what Screwtape implies when he concludes his letter this way: "*Even of his sins* the Enemy does not want him to think too much: once they are repented, the sooner the man turns his attention outward, the better the Enemy is pleased."[6]

A question we have to ask ourselves here is this: when we are overly distressed by our own weaknesses and sins, are our motives always pure? Is it possible that our interior anguish is not just over offending our loving God, *but about the collapse of the ideal version of ourselves which we have grown to cherish so much*?

In other words, sometimes when we fall and are terribly distraught, we are really thinking, "How could *I* have done that?" In those moments, we witness the fracturing of the idealized version of ourselves; and to this extent, the root of our anguish is actually (and ironically) *pride*. Jacques Philippe describes this dynamic well:

> [T]he sadness and the discouragement that we feel regarding our failures and our faults are rarely pure; they are not very often the simple pain of having offended God. They are in good part mixed with pride. We are not sad and discouraged so much because God was offended, but because the ideal image that we have of ourselves has been brutally shaken. *Our pain is very often that of wounded pride.*[7]

5. Ibid., 71–72. See Lewis, *Mere Christianity*, 125, 128, and Lewis, *Great Divorce*, 86.

6. Ibid., 73, emphasis added.

7. Philippe, *Searching for and Maintaining Peace*, 58, emphasis added.

This is exactly what Screwtape is getting at when he says *"even of his own sins"* the Enemy does not want the patient to think too much. Yes, we should repent of our sins; but there is a sense in which when we fall—if we know we are children of God who are broken and fallen—our attitude should be something like, "I'm sorry, Lord, there I go again—I'm broken; help me, Lord."

What makes a saint is not someone who just "tries" really hard; it's someone who has gone to the divine physician and shown him *all* of their wounds and has allowed Jesus to enter into every crevice of their being. Here, humility is the door that only *we* can open—a door that makes real healing possible, allowing the grace of God to truly enter our lives and transform us from within.

We must let go of the "idealized version" of ourselves and let God love us as we are. Yes, we will make improvement, for God's grace can move mountains and bring about unfathomable changes—just look at the apostles. But for that to happen, we must first let go of ourselves; if we wish to enter into this great dance of love, we must forget ourselves.

Humility helps to make this happen by turning our attention outward, in love of God and neighbor. And this includes having the humility to accept our weaknesses and present them *as* weaknesses to our loving Father; in this sense, humility is the first step not just to loving our neighbor, but to truly loving ourselves as well.

We must resist the temptation to seek perfection and *then* present ourselves to God; rather, we must first go to him precisely in our weakness. This type of humility and confidence in God's love creates an armor that the devil cannot penetrate. And conversely, without this type of humility and confidence in God's love, even the most heroic of virtues won't fend off the attacks of the Evil One.

The Accuser

Interestingly, the Hebrew word *satan* actually means "to accuse" or "the accuser" (see Zech 3:1–5). In the midst of temptation, Satan is our buddy, coaxing us along and enticing us to sin. But when we fall, his tactic changes: he becomes the "accuser," seeking to bury us in shame and keep us from the throne of mercy.[8] Here is where our "wounded pride"—our sadness at coming face to face with our brokenness, and our sadness at the crumbling of the idealized version of ourselves—makes us especially vulnerable to his attack. If we cling to this perfected version of ourselves, we will be extremely susceptible—especially when that ideal image starts to crack, as it inevitably will.

But if we have the humility not only to not be excessively concerned with our strengths and accomplishments, but also to accept our limitations and weaknesses (and let go of the idealized version of ourselves), then we become impervious to the devil's onslaught. This type of humility (and bold confidence in the love and mercy of God) attaches us to God so firmly that literally nothing can separate us from the love of Christ (see Rom 8:35).

It's for this reason that Screwtape is so concerned with humility; for a distorted humility he can work with, but a true and sincere humility that opens us up to the love of God, neighbor, *and even ourselves* is a fortress he finds impenetrable. Indeed, very often the whole battle hangs in the balance right here—and Screwtape knows it.

In the next chapter, we continue to pursue some of these same themes, with a particular focus on anxiety and how anxiety turns us inward. We will also treat common sources of anxiety, such as the suffering of our loved ones and discernment—that is, the anguish we often feel when trying to discern God's call for our lives.

---

8. See my *John Paul II to Aristotle and Back Again*, 44.

Chapter 8

Letter 15: Anxiety and False Peace

SCREWTAPE BEGINS THIS LETTER by noting that the Enemy (God) wants us to attend chiefly to two things—*eternity* and the *present*: "For the Present is the point at which time touches eternity."[1]

Screwtape's goal, then, is the exact opposite—to get the patient's attention off of eternity and the present and engrossed in either the *past* or the *future*.[2]

As he recounts, sometimes a widow or a scholar is firmly in the grip of the *past*—longing for a time that has gone by—but for Screwtape, getting human beings into the clutches of an anxiety-riddled and unknown *future* is "far better."[3] As Screwtape writes: "[N]early all vices are rooted in the future. Gratitude looks to the past and love to the present; fear, avarice, lust, and ambition look ahead."[4]

But what about planning for the future? Doesn't God want us to provide for ourselves and those within our care?

Screwtape acknowledges this point. And what we see here is that focusing on the present is really an *attitude* of surrender, detachment, and confidence in God; it is not a call to negligence and irresponsibility, but an exhortation to do our part in all that we can—and then entrust all things into the hands of Almighty God. Screwtape, on the other hand, wants the man to be overly pained by anxiety, and ready and willing to break God's commands in the present, if by this chance he might be able to avoid whatever he is fearful of. Screwtape writes:

1. Lewis, *Screwtape Letters*, 75.
2. Ibid., 76.
3. Ibid.
4. Ibid.

To be sure, the Enemy wants men to think of the Future too—just so much as is necessary for *now* planning the acts of justice or charity which will probably be their duty tomorrow. The duty of planning the morrow's work is *today's* duty. . . . He does not want men to give the Future their hearts, to place their treasure in it. *We do.* His ideal is a man who, having worked all day for the good of posterity (if that is his vocation) washes his mind of the whole subject, commits the issue to Heaven, and returns at once to the patience or gratitude demanded by the moment that is passing over him. But we want a man hag-ridden by the Future—haunted by visions of an imminent heaven or hell upon earth—ready to break the Enemy's commands in the present if by doing so we make him think he can attain the one or avert the other. . . . We want a whole race perpetually in pursuit of the rainbow's end, never honest, nor kind, nor happy *now.*[5]

A False Peace

Screwtape goes on to discuss the patient, noting that he may be at peace in the present, but only in a tenuous way. If his "peace" is just because things happen to be going well, then he is still within the demon's grasp. In Screwtape's words: "He may be untroubled about the Future, not because he is concerned with the Present, but because he has persuaded himself that the Future is going to be agreeable."[6]

For Screwtape, if this is his source of "peace"—and not detachment and confidence in God—then he is only setting himself up for "disappointment . . . when his false hopes are dashed."[7] Most likely, the patient is at peace "because his health is good and he is enjoying his work."[8]

5. Ibid., 77–78, emphasis original.
6. Ibid., 78.
7. Ibid.
8. Ibid., 79.

As we know all too well, it's a lot easier to live in the present when things are going well; and if present success is our source of interior peace, then we have not yet tapped into the "peace that the world cannot give"—the peace that only comes from knowing Jesus Christ personally, in a living and dynamic way.

This is easier said than done. But what Screwtape is unwittingly teaching us is that our source of peace can't be something external; it can't simply be how things happen to be going—because that is far too fragile and can easily change. True peace has to be rooted in our confidence in God and a conviction in what life is ultimately about—only here do we find a peace that is not easily shaken.

For the rest of the chapter, we will step away from Screwtape and continue this theme of peace and anxiety. First, we will look at how anxiety affects our capacity to love. Then we will turn to some of the most common reasons why we lose our peace—namely, the suffering of our loved ones and our attempts to discern God's will for our lives.

Anxiety—What's Love Got to Do with It?

So, why is anxiety such a big deal in the spiritual life? Why do so many writers speak of it in such a serious manner, as Screwtape does here?

As we have seen throughout, God desires our outward orientation—for us to turn outward in love of him and neighbor. But anxiety directly thwarts this goal because it decidedly turns us inward.

I'm sure we've all been there before, when we were really anxious and consumed with worry—how available were we to those around us? When we were so overtaken and preoccupied with our own concerns, how much did we truly enter into the world of those around us?

For my part, when I've experienced such moments of all-consuming worry and anxiety, even though I was physically present, I was not *really there*; my mind was constantly elsewhere and I was really only concerned with myself—my projects and my problems.

Here we see that maintaining peace of mind and heart is not just about our own serenity and being able to deal with life: *our peace of heart directly affects our ability to love.* That is, our interior peace enables us to be more and more other-centered and *available* to those around us.

Anxiety, on the other hand, turns us inward—we can only think about ourselves and our own concerns. At some point, we have to turn over what we cannot control to the Lord—and it is this surrender which frees us to love and truly enter into the world of those around us, as Jacques Philippe writes: "[O]nly this peace of heart truly liberates us from ourselves, increases our sensitivity to others and renders us available to our fellow man."[9]

Further, if sanctity is the fruit of God's work in us, Philippe rightly notes that the more we surrender our lives in peace to God, the more efficaciously he can work through us. And conversely, our anxiety and need for absolute "control" tends to obstruct his movement in us.

In order to illustrate this point, Philippe uses the image of a lake: if the surface is tranquil, it better reflects the light of the sun; if troubled, less so. The same is true of God's movement in us:

> The more our soul is peaceful and tranquil, the more God is reflected in it; the more His image expresses itself in us, the more His grace acts through us. On the other hand, if our soul is agitated and troubled, the grace of God is able to act only with much greater difficulty.[10]

True and False Compassion

This peace might be attainable when it comes to our own lives and our own struggles, but what about the trials and suffering of those we love? This is where our peace is especially tested. But out of love

---

9. Philippe, *Searching for and Maintaining Peace*, 7.
10. Ibid., 5.

for our friends and family, shouldn't we be distressed and worried about their plight?

Of course, the answer is "yes." But Philippe offers deep spiritual insight here. First, we must reckon with the fact that God's ways are not our ways—we see only through a glass darkly and do not have God's vantage point. And while we believe that God is always at work—even through evil and suffering (see Gen 50:20)—we must also accept that we may never fully understand the reasons for this or that suffering. In short, we trust God first, and then we try to understand second—not the other way around.

For Philippe, true compassion in these circumstances—as a Christian virtue—is motivated by *love* and not *fear*. And this love has to take into account much more than our limited perspective; that is, this love must take into account the good for our loved ones—*as God sees it, in light of his designs*. Philippe writes:

> In order for it to be a true Christian virtue, compassion for others must proceed from love (which consists in desiring the good of others, *in the light of God and in accord with His designs*) and not from fear (fear of suffering, fear of losing something). But, in fact, all too often our attitude toward those around us who are suffering is more conditioned by fear than love. *One thing is certain: God loves our dear ones infinitely more than we do, and infinitely better.*[11]

I think we know in our minds that God cares for our loved ones even more than we do, but it is exceedingly difficult to let this truth sink into our hearts. Nonetheless, it is something we must ponder in faith. And very often, hanging on to this truth is the only thing that will get us through such dark times.

Moreover, Philippe offers an additional benefit to this true compassion, which is motivated by love and not fear: our loved ones who are suffering need people around them who exude peace, joy, and confidence; that is, they don't need us to communicate our anxiety and lack of confidence in God to them. In fact,

11. Ibid., 47–48, emphasis added.

sometimes the one bearing the suffering does so with more peace and tranquility than those around him. Philippe writes:

> Our brothers and sisters who suffer need peaceful, confident, and joyful people around them and will be helped much more effectively by them than by those who are preoccupied or anxious. Our false compassion [motivated by fear] often only adds to their sadness and distress. It is not a source of peace and hope for those who suffer.[12]

Of course, we should do what is in our power to relieve the suffering of those around us. But much of the spiritual struggle here concerns the attitude with which we do such things: "It is our duty to do these things, to be sure. But we should do them in a spirit of peace and confident abandonment into the hands of God."[13]

God loves us more than we love ourselves, and the same is true of our loved ones. His ways are not our ways. And we know that "here, we have no lasting city" (Heb 13:14)—this is not our true and ultimate home. This is the perspective we can never forget.

It takes great courage to love others—to seek their good—especially, as Philippe writes, "in the light of God and in accordance with His designs."[14] Too often, we can't get past *our* plans and *our* designs. But true Christian love and compassion must try—as we much as we are able—to see things from God's perspective, tending to our loved ones out of love and not fear; for they are in the hands of one much greater than ourselves—one who loves them much more than we do.

Discerning God's Will

We know that one much greater than ourselves holds and directs our future as well. Sometimes our sense for what God wants of us is clear and unmistakable; these are our "burning bush"

12. Ibid., 48.
13. Ibid., 49.
14. Ibid., 47.

moments—and they are moments of great grace and peace that we should joyfully embrace. But frequently, we become anxious when we are unable to understand God's plan for our lives with any kind of confidence and conviction. Often, it seems like there is more than one "good" and "holy" option—sometimes we are not sure exactly what God wants of us and how he might be leading us. What do we do then?

First, we need to make sure we have really *prayed* about it—not just *thought* about it. And as we mentioned earlier, quiet mental prayer—where we really *listen* to the voice of God—is key to discerning his will; it is essential if we are going to align our hearts with the movement of his providence.

Second, we should seek *counsel* from spiritual leaders and mentors; here, if we can, we should seek a variety of counselors and be leery of the temptation to seek counsel only from people whom we know are likely tell us what we want to hear. We have to let God work and not seek to manipulate the situation.

Third, it is always helpful to be *patient*. Sometimes in these situations, we act in an immature way—like children who want an answer *now*. Part of the growth that God wants for us in these situations often lies in the *process*—this is what we tend to forget. If it were always easy to discover God's will, in a real sense we would never grow up as Christians.

In my experience, very often God reveals himself in the "daily grind." In other words, we often think that a few intense prayer sessions will give us unmistakable clarity. And sometimes it happens just like that. But often, as we know, this doesn't happen. Often, the answer comes not in one or two intense prayer sessions, but in six months of just going about our daily lives—in living our lives well in the little things and not obsessing over the decision. This is the *process* of Christian maturation, which we sometimes inadvertently seek to short-circuit in our demands for an immediate answer.

Fourth, in my experience, it has always been helpful to look for the *recurring* thought. That is, we have to distinguish between our varying *moods* and God's promptings on our heart. Sometimes we get excited about this or that prospect, but it doesn't have staying power—it erupts quickly and then goes away. But if we have a bit of holy patience here, we will often see that, though several options are appealing, we keep coming back to one in particular. This takes time, but I have found that this *recurring* thought or inspiration is often a steady and sure sign of God's will for my life.

Finally, as we proceed to a decision point, we want to make our decision in a state of equilibrium—that is, neither too high nor too low. When we're really high or really low, we don't see things clearly; we tend to act impulsively—either diving in without due discretion (in a high moment) or giving up too easily (in a low moment). Here, the Evil One will seek to confuse us and destroy our peace. But if we have patience, we'll be able to wade through the peaks and valleys and come to a confident mature decision.

But what if, after all of this, we still aren't sure? Would God ever leave us in the dark like that?

For my part, much of the anxiety—especially with young people, say, in discerning marriage or ministry—is due to the fact that they often assume God would *never* leave them in the dark; therefore, when this happens (as it inevitably does), they assume that *there must be something wrong*—that they must have missed something and are in danger of acting contrary to God's will. In other words, we often assume that the "burning bush" is the *norm*—that God *normally* gives unmistakable clarity.

On some things, we do have clarity: while on the one hand, God does work through our desires, on the other hand, if we seek to do something contrary to the moral law, then we know something is off. That is, we have absolute clarity on what *not* to do. But how do we discern positively what *to do*?

As I alluded to above, sometimes God simply wants us to mature; it takes great guts and courage to step out and make a decision in faith *without absolute certainty*. And as we do, we grow in our ability to make Christian decisions in the future.

So, if we've *prayed*, sought *counsel*, and have been *patient*, then we should simply "jump." Here, the devil will seek to paralyze us, getting us to feel like we can't decide until we have some absolute certainty—and then life passes us by. For not to decide eventually *is* to decide. In our fear of not being certain—in our fear of being wrong—we often simply fail to act; we fail to have the courage to act. At this point, we have to trust that God has worked through the ordinary channels of our prayer and counsel to reveal to us what we needed to know. We have to have confidence and trust in God—we cannot second-guess ourselves forever.

Now, if we haven't taken the above steps (prayer, counsel, patience), *then we should be nervous.* But if we have, then we need to trust that God can always "write straight with our crooked lines."

In sum, there is immense growth that occurs when we sincerely pray (over a period of time), seek counsel, and wait upon the Lord in patience—and then make a decision in courage and faith, even though we lack certainty. All too often, we are oblivious to the importance of the *process* and the growth this brings about— a process that greatly matures both our faith and courage. Once again, Philippe describes this dynamic well:

> [O]ften the Lord speaks to us in diverse ways and makes us understand in a clear way how we must act. . . . *But, it may happen that the Lord does not respond to us. And this is completely normal.* Sometimes, He simply leaves us free and sometimes, for reasons of His own, He does not manifest Himself. It is good to know this, because it often happens that people, for fear of making a mistake, of not doing the will of God, seek at any price to have an answer. They increase their reflections, their prayers, they open the Bible ten times looking for a text in order to obtain the desired enlightenment. And all this is troubling and disquieting more than anything else. . . . When the Lord leaves us in incertitude, we must quietly accept it.[15]

Philippe goes on to discuss this desire for absolute certainty, noting how it sometimes masks pride and a lack of confidence in God, and sometimes it simply masks an inability on our part to take responsibility for our decisions—a fear of having to decide for ourselves:

15. Ibid., 72.

For one thing, this desire to know what God wants sometimes hides a difficulty in enduring a situation of incertitude. *We want to be released from having to decide by
ourselves. But, frequently, the will of the Lord is that we do
decide for ourselves, even if we are not absolutely sure.* . . . In
effect, in this capacity to decide in incertitude . . . there is
an attitude of confidence and abandonment. . . . We would
love to be infallible, to never be wrong, but there is a lot of
pride in this desire and there is also the fear of being judged
by others. . . . [T]he Lord loves him more who knows how
to decide for himself without equivocating, even when he
is uncertain, and who abandons himself with confidence
to God as to the consequences, rather than the one who
torments his spirit unceasingly in an effort to know what
God expects of him and who never decides. . . . Perfection-
ism doesn't have much to do with sanctity.[16]

We have to believe that God can and does work through the
messiness of our lives and the clumsiness of our prayer. If we seek
him sincerely, we should be confident that he will bring us home.
If we have done what we can, if we have done our part—in prayer,
counsel, and patient endurance—then at some point we simply
have to "jump" and trust our Heavenly Father to catch us. After all,
he cares far more about our happiness and our salvation than we
do. Therefore, we need not fear; and at some point, we have to surrender and abandon to him our ability (or inability) to discern his
will. This is part of the great drama of human life: we have a Father
in heaven who loves us; if we do our part, we need not fear—he
will bring us home.

In the next chapter, once again, the little things show up as
matters of immense importance—here, the issue is gluttony. For
Screwtape, this vice is about far more than the quantity of our in-
take. In fact, by the end of this chapter, we will see the intimate
relationship between social justice and individual ethics: for how
can we have a just *society*, unless we first have just and virtuous
individuals who make up that society?

16. Ibid., 74–75.

Chapter 9

Letter 17: Gluttony and Charity

WHETHER IT'S CHIPOTLE, STEAK, pizza, or Thanksgiving, as Americans, we love our food, just about as much as we love football. And we certainly love meals for more reasons than just the pleasures of the palate: festive occasions and dining bring people together—not just to enjoy a meal, but to enjoy fellowship with one another.

Most of us are aware that overeating probably isn't a good habit to get into; but in this letter, Screwtape points out something rooted in the Christian moral and spiritual tradition—namely, that the vice of gluttony concerns more than just *quantity*. Besides gluttony of excess, being overly picky or being overly concerned with having the nicest or best quality of food have also been seen as expressions of this vice.[1]

This letter concerns the patient's mother (to whom we referred in chapter 1) and her habit of falling into a certain form of gluttony—a gluttony of delicacy. While her small quantities deceive her, she is nonetheless governed by her palate. Screwtape writes:

> She would be astonished—one day, I hope, *will* be—to learn that her whole life is enslaved to this kind of sensuality, which is quite concealed from her by the fact that the quantities involved are small.[2]

It's not just the food and her desire to have things prepared a certain way; it's also (and even primarily) how this desire affects

1. Aquinas, *Summa Theologica*, II-IIae, q. 148, a. 4.
2. Lewis, *Screwtape Letters,* 87, emphasis original.

the way in which she interacts with others. Her determination to have things a certain way—and her frustration when things are not to her liking—dramatically undermine her ability to be kind and considerate. Screwtape explains:

> [W]hat do quantities matter, provided we use a human belly and palate to produce querulousness, impatience, uncharitableness, and self-concern. . . . She is a positive terror to hostesses and servants. . . . Because what she wants is smaller and less costly than what has been set before her, she never recognizes as gluttony her determination to get what she wants, however troublesome it may be to others. At the very moment of indulging her appetite she believes that she is practicing temperance.[3]

Small World, Overbearing Palate

Screwtape goes on to describe how the patient's mother has a recollection of "properly" prepared meals from the past—with which nothing in the present can compare. But Screwtape explains that—unbeknownst to her—in previous years she had a fuller life, with the result that her palate was more easily satisfied:

> The woman is in what may be called the "All-I-want" state of mind. *All* she wants is a cup of tea properly made, or an egg properly boiled, or a slice of bread properly toasted. But she never finds any servant or any friend who does these simple things "properly"—because her "properly" conceals an insatiable demand for the exact, and almost impossible, palatal pleasures which she imagines she remembers from the past; a past described by her as "the days when you could get good servants" *but known to us as the days when her senses were more easily pleased and she had pleasures of other kinds which made her less dependent on those of the table.*[4]

3. Ibid., 87–88.
4. Ibid., 88–89, first emphasis original, added in last sentence.

As we have mentioned earlier, we still speak of "comfort food," a phrase that shows our recognition that eating can be a compensation for an interior sadness and depression. In a real sense, man cannot live without pleasure and joy; and if he cannot find it in more meaningful things—God, friendship, and love of neighbor—then he'll look for it wherever he can (e.g., food, drink, and sex).

It's Not Hurting Anyone

In our culture, we often think about morality this way: "*If it's not hurting anyone, then it can't be wrong*." And there's a reason why many think that.

But what we see in a small way with the mother is that a lack of temperance—the virtue that moderates our desire for bodily pleasure (e.g., food, drink, and sex)—will eventually end up becoming a nuisance to others. That is, our ability (or inability) to attain self-mastery—and rise above our desires—directly affects our ability to love others.

As we said, it's not just about food. Whatever it is, if we are so determined to have it—or to have it a certain way—then how will we react when it's not available? Saint Paul describes "covetousness" as "idolatry" (Col 3:5); that is, if we covet something—if we want it so badly—it becomes a "god" that we worship; it becomes the ultimate end toward which our activities and desires tend. And when that happens, we set ourselves up to be "put out" when that desire can't be fulfilled—in which case we become less and less pleasant to be around. Screwtape sees this same dynamic taking place with the man as well (the woman's son):

> [H]owever you approach it, the great thing is to bring him into the state in which the denial of any one indulgence—it matters not which, champagne or tea, *sole Colbert* or cigarettes—"puts him out," *for then his charity, justice, and obedience are all at your mercy.*[5]

5. Ibid., 90, emphasis added.

Here again, Screwtape sees clearly the link between one's self-control—the ability to govern one's own desires and passions—and our capacity to be kind and loving toward others. In fact, in another work, *Mere Christianity*, C. S. Lewis captured this relationship in his classic metaphor of humanity as a fleet of ships. So, in order to better see this relationship between social and individual ethics, we will now take up this analogy.

Fleet of Ships

Lewis describes morality in terms of a fleet of ships, laying out three stipulations for the success (and happiness) of their journey: (1) don't collide; (2) each ship must be seaworthy; (3) all the ships must be going in the same general direction.[6] We'll discuss the first two here.

The first stipulation is the obvious one; this is the most common meaning of morality for people today—basically a sense of "fair play" or justice with respect to one another. It's the social aspect of morality, the "golden rule" as taught by Jesus. It's this stipulation that people are referring to when they say: "If it's not hurting anybody, then it can't be wrong."

The second stipulation is something prized by the classical and Christian moral tradition, but certainly not to the neglect of the first: each ship must be seaworthy in that each individual must attend to his or her own moral development—here, in our example, the ability to have self-control and self-mastery.

Lewis's point is this: if a ship is not seaworthy—say, if its motor doesn't work, or its steering apparatus is faulty—*then it will collide with another ship*. In other words, the first stipulation ("don't collide") can't be kept without the second ("each ship must be seaworthy"); and it's only the second—the seaworthiness of each ship—that makes possible the safekeeping of the first—not colliding.

In effect, Lewis is saying that you can't have *social* morality (don't collide) without *individual* morality (be seaworthy). If we

---

6. Lewis, *Mere Christianity*, 71–73.

don't have individuals who can rise above their own self-interest or desires for the sake of a greater good, then how can we expect individuals to care for the environment, or be interested in the poor whom they may not know—or the unborn who cannot even cry to defend themselves?

For this reason, growing in interior self-mastery and virtue is prerequisite to being able to make a gift of ourselves in love and ensure justice for all. We'll never have a just society if we don't first have just and upright individuals.

In small ways and over time, our character becomes more and more fixed in one direction or another. Even something as seemingly insignificant as the way we conduct ourselves during meals can, over time, affect our ability to love; if we're not careful, it can reduce our capacity to be other-centered in an outward and loving way.

And it's certainly not just about eating. Any addictive behavior—whether it be drugs, alcohol, or pornography—eventually reaps destructive consequences on those around us. The husband or wife who uses pornography: to whom do they make love—the images they have engrossed themselves in, or their spouse? In this sense, there are no merely "private" sins, for the way in which we continue to form our character will eventually impact those around us. And especially with pornography, where such addictions often form at a young age, there is great need to take this moral formation seriously from the very beginning. As Lewis might put it, if I'm going to avoid "colliding" in the future, I must first train myself to become "seaworthy."

In the next chapter, we turn to the "philosophy of hell," in contrast to its heavenly counterpart. As we'll see, the philosophy of hell is built on the assumption that true love is not possible—indeed, it replaces love with envy. We'll contrast this with true love, and then we'll pursue the root and source of that love in God himself: for the "philosophy of heaven" and our call to love is rooted in God's own Trinitarian nature. As we'll see, the more we understand *who* God is, the better we understand what he has done for us.

Chapter 10

Letters 18 and 19: The Philosophy of Hell and the Mystery of Love

THE "PHILOSOPHY OF HELL," Screwtapes writes, "rests on the recognition of the axiom that one thing is not another thing."[1] What Screwtape means here is that the philosophy of hell is based on *competition*: my good cannot be your good, and vice versa. Therefore, it's always a zero-sum game—if you're up, I'm down. As Screwtape says, "'To be' *means* 'to be in competition.'"[2]

For Screwtape, the Enemy's (i.e., God's) philosophy, on the other hand, is a contradiction: "Things are to be many, yet somehow also one. The good of one self is to be the good of another. This impossibility He calls *love*."[3]

True love unites two in one mind and heart, such that the other's good becomes my good—the other's victories, sorrows, needs, dreams, and aspirations become my own. Love, as Screwtape clearly sees, *unites*, whereas the philosophy of hell inherently *divides*, insisting that there can be no true union between two separate individuals since the two are by necessity in competitive strife with one another.

Envy Is Diabolical

Screwtape's discussion here is eerily reminiscent of what the Christian tradition has understood by envy. While today we often use

1. Lewis, *Screwtape Letters*, 94, emphasis original.
2. Ibid., 94, emphasis original.
3. Ibid., emphasis original.

the terms jealousy and envy interchangeably, the concepts can be distinguished. Envy is *sorrow* at the good of another (or rejoicing at the misfortune of another),[4] whereas jealousy is simply desiring the good of another.

This may seem like hairsplitting, but the distinction can be profound. Jealousy can be neutral, perhaps even good in the right setting; whereas envy will always be bad.

Take, for example, a basketball team: let's say I am jealous of some of my teammates who are getting more playing time than I am, or perhaps I am jealous of their ball-handling skills or shooting ability. This recognition on my part may cause me to reflect on how much harder they are working than I am, either at practice or in the off season; in other words, my desiring their good may lead me to better emulate their work habits, in hopes of achieving the same good. Here, I am jealous (i.e., I desire the same good they have acquired), but I don't necessarily resent them for having attained this good; I just want the same for myself.

Envy, on the other hand, isn't simply about my desiring what they have. Envy is precisely my *resentment that they have it*. Envy gives rise to the attitude, *"If I can't have it, I don't want anyone else to have it either."* In terms of the basketball analogy, envy might lead me to rejoice when one of my teammates gets injured (i.e., rejoicing at their misfortune). It represents a zero-sum attitude, in which case their good is necessarily my loss and vice versa.

In this situation, I cannot ever be happy for others—because envy *is* sorrow at their good. Here, we see that envy is diametrically opposed to love. As was said above, love unites two minds and hearts, such that the good of one becomes the good of the other; whereas envy divides—much as Screwtape said above: "to be *means* to be in competition." Envy destroys friendship because it hinders people from truly uniting in communion, and it often gives rise to backbiting and gossip. After all, the only way for me to climb upward is for others to be brought down—and in this context, it doesn't really matter how they fall.[5]

4. Aquinas, *Summa Theologica*, II-IIae, q. 36, a. 1.

5. For more on envy, see my *John Paul II to Aristotle and Back Again*, 42–43.

Overcoming Envy

One way to try to combat envy (and gossip) is to actively praise the very people of whom we're most prone to be envious. Very often with virtues and vices, we can't simply stop doing the bad; *we must practice the opposite virtue*—we must overcome the bad habit with the good. If we actively seek to admire—in the presence of others—the very person with whom we tend to feel we're in competition, we will eventually see the grip of envy loosen from our hearts.

Secondly, envy tends to flow from insecurity—we're unsure of ourselves, so we resent others who have what we want. The more we come to grips with who we are—with respect to both our talents *and* our limitations—the more the clutches of envy lose their hold on us. The person who is grateful and is finding their role in God's plan tends to feel secure and confident, and therefore not as prone to envy. We need to actualize *our* fullest potential—not somebody else's. Keeping our attention here on ourselves, as opposed to constantly comparing and competing with those around us, helps to curb envy.

My two oldest kids are both boys and are just a little over a year apart, and they're always competing with one another—usually in a healthy manner. But I always stress that it's not just about beating the other guy; the real question is: are *you* getting better? In other words, I stress to them that the real competition is with *yourself*—and if you're improving, that's all that matters.

The more we focus on ourselves—with gratitude for the gifts we do possess and acceptance of our limitations—the less prone to envy we become. The more we are secure, whole, and confident in ourselves, the freer we are to love and to truly enter into the lives of those around us.

As we've seen throughout, God wants us to take our attention off ourselves and turn outward in love. But *envy represents a sorrowful turn inward*; we're only concerned with ourselves—with what we don't have (or with what others *do* have). Thus, envy thwarts love: I cannot unite myself with the other, rejoicing in their good as if it were my own, since envy inherently divides—it divides minds and hearts (since the other's good is precisely my *loss*). And in so doing, it becomes a toxin to real friendship—and at the same, to joy as well.

Now we will step away from Screwtape and explore further the great mystery of love and its source in God himself and what this means for salvation. As we have seen, the devil cannot comprehend love—it doesn't make sense—and the demonic substitute is envy. This difference between God and the devil—between love and envy—permeates everything about the Christian story. And this is for good reason: God *is* love; that is, the mystery of God's love for us goes down into the very depths of *who* he is.

As a forewarning, some of this material ventures into deep waters of theology; but it is certainly relevant and worth the effort, because the very root and depth of our faith—the mystery of who God is in himself eternally—greatly illumines the mystery of salvation and what God has done for us. Thus, even though it is difficult, this is something the devil certainly wants to keep far from our minds and hearts. He does not want us to know *who* God is—that he *is* love—for the devil's lie always and everywhere is that God cannot and does not really love us.

A God Who Is Love—in Creation

As St. John writes, "God is love" (1 John 4:8), and we are made in the image of this God (Gen 1:26–28)—that's why love is so central to the Christian story and the overall Christian message. As we'll see in a moment, God *is* utter gift—a truth that illumines the whole of God's plan and explains why he calls us to make a gift of our lives in love to others.

In a real sense, part of the gospel is that God doesn't need us. This may sound shocking, but it follows from God's very nature. That is, God doesn't create out of *need*—for needy love is always an imperfect kind of love. Rather, our God—who is in need of nothing and has every perfection within himself—creates simply to *share* that goodness with us. As the Christian tradition has often said, "the good is self-diffusive."[6] In other words, the good has an inherent orientation outward; it doesn't want to be held in—much like when we see a great movie, we want to tell people about it. God, then, did not *have* to create—he did so freely; but still, it is exceedingly fitting that he did create—for how could such Infinite Goodness hold itself in?

God is utter *gift*. He gives himself in creation, not out of need, but to share what he has eternally with us. And this gift continues and climaxes with the sending of the Son and the Spirit: the Son dies our death and rises to new life—not merely to atone for our sins, but to infuse his divine life into us. The gift of the Holy Spirit is the culmination of God going outside of himself and pouring himself out in creation. All things come forth from God, and through the Son and the Spirit they return to God in glory.

A God Who Is Love—in Himself as Trinity

This pouring out of himself in the works of creation and redemption points to an even deeper mystery within God himself. While there is one God, he exists as three distinct persons. These persons do not disrupt the unity of God's nature; and conversely, the unity of God's nature does not preclude the real distinction of persons within God. That is, there are not three gods—nor are "Father," "Son," and "Holy Spirit" simply three masks worn by one entity. God is one *and* yet three distinct persons. But how can this be?

As we'll see in a moment, *love* finds a way: the mystery of God's unity and plurality flows from the great mystery of love within God himself. This is certainly not a math problem, and it is nothing our natural reason could ever have come to on its own; it is in the truest sense of the word a Christian "mystery," revealed only in faith. We believe it because we *trust* the God who has revealed it to us.

What we see in this ancient faith is that God is inherently *dynamic*, not static: there is a dynamic and loving communication

---

6. This phrase is often attributed to St. Bonaventure.

of the divine nature within God—and this flows essentially from God's nature. The Father eternally begets the Son. In the creed, we say the Son is "begotten, not made." It's analogous to human begetting—that is, *like* and *unlike*. If I make a statue, the statue does not share my human nature—this is the distinction between begetting and making: what is "made" is of a different nature than the maker. If I beget children, on the other hand, I communicate my human nature to them; they are of the same nature as myself. This is how the Son's eternal begetting is *like* human begetting: when we say that the Son is "begotten," we are saying that he is of the same nature as the Father. The difference between the begetting of the Eternal Son and our begetting is that human begetting occurs in time, in which case a human father exists first and then his children later. But the Son is *eternally* begotten of the Father, and so the time element must be removed—in which case, there never was a "time" when the Son did not exist.

With the Son's begetting, the Father and the Son exchange in a bond of love, and this bond of love is the dynamic exchange that gives rise to the Holy Spirit; that is, the love between the Father and the Son is so real and so profound that it is a *person* proceeding forth from them both. The Holy Spirit is not a "force," but is the third *person* of the Trinity, flowing dynamically from this union of love. Again, these are *eternal* relations, so we must remove the time element. In these three relations, we have a total communication of the divine nature—from Father to Son, and from the Father and Son to the Holy Spirit. We have here an eternal bond of love.

Thus, the three persons are *one* with respect to the divine nature; they are *three* with respect to how they communicate and receive this divine nature from one another—that is, they are three in their *relations* to one another. The Son proceeds from the Father; the Holy Spirit proceeds from the love between the Father and the Son; while the Father does not proceed—he is ordered inherently and essentially to the begetting of the Son (which gives rise to the Holy Spirit through their bond of love). Notice, again, that God is inherently *relational*—that's why St. John can say, "God *is* love"—not as a mere metaphor, but as the ultimate reality of who God is.

To use another analogy closer to home: while man is made in the image of God individually, the Genesis text goes on to say, "male and female he made them" (Gen 1:27). In other words, man reflects God's image not only individually, but also *communally*—especially in the marriage bond.[7] For in marriage, when the husband gives himself totally to his wife and the wife gives herself totally to her husband, their love becomes so real and so profound that often nine months later they have to give it a name! That is, in the union of the marital act, their total self-giving becomes life-giving. And so the union of the two (the husband and wife) gives rise to a third (the child), through a bond of love; and this life-giving exchange becomes an image of God's eternal life-giving bond of love within himself—as Father, Son, and Holy Spirit. In other words, God *is* the Eternal Family—the eternal communion of persons—from which the human family takes its likeness.

We are made for communion because we are made in the image of this God who *is* communion. We are made for love because the source of all reality—in whose image we have been made—*is* an eternal and dynamic exchange of love.

Divine Sonship

God's reason for revealing this mystery of his inner life to us isn't simply to humble and astonish our rational faculties. Rather, as the nineteenth-century theologian Matthias Scheeben taught, God revealed this eternal begetting within himself in order to show us the ultimate model and pattern of our destiny.[8]

That is, God can make us his sons and daughters because he *is* Father and Son by nature. God can communicate his divine nature to us by grace because he *is* the eternal dynamic communication of the divine nature in himself. And so what God does in time flows from who he is eternally.

---

7. See John Paul II, *Man and Woman He Created Them*.

8. Scheeben, *Mysteries of Christianity*, 141–42.

Further, as Scheeben taught, the sending of the Son and the Spirit *prolong these eternal processions within God into time.*[9] This movement, then, is about God pouring himself out and inviting us into his own inner life—a life that would have been inaccessible to us apart from God's own free initiative. That is, moral perfection could not earn one drop of this divine life, so understood.

Salvation, therefore, is not just about forgiveness of sin; even more, salvation is about becoming sons and daughters of God in and through the Son and the Spirit. Salvation is sharing in the Son's eternal relation to the Father: what the Son has eternally *by nature*, he has shared with us *by grace*. This is why salvation doesn't end with the cross, for "he was raised for our justification" (Rom 4:25). God became man in Jesus Christ in order to take on our sin and die our death; but it didn't stop there: *he wanted to infuse his own divine life into us.*[10] That's why St. Peter can say that, through Christ, we have become "partakers of the divine nature" (2 Pet 1:4).

God is utter gift—internally within the Trinity, and externally going outside of himself in creation and redemption. God *is* a dynamic exchange of life and love, and he invites us to enjoy this dynamic exchange eternally. In creation and especially in the sending of the Son and the Spirit, he seeks to bring us into his inner heart of life and love. Salvation, then, is not just about atonement: it brings us into this eternal family of love, within the very heart of the Trinity. Salvation, in other words, is about becoming a child of God—a son or daughter in the Eternal Son.

This is what the devil will never understand: namely, that God is love and that he gives without holding back—and that our destiny is to share in in this Trinitarian exchange of love forever.

The Devil's Lie

Since Screwtape cannot believe in the real possibility of love (because that would contradict the first principle of the philosophy

9. Ibid., 157, 160, 179–80, 313, 359–60, 384–85.

10. See Meconi and Olson, eds., *Called to Be the Children of God*, and Hofter, ed., *Divinization.*

of hell), he cannot comprehend what in the world God is up to. Alluding to the fall of Satan, Screwtape writes:

> What does He [God] stand to make out of them [humans]? That is the insoluble question. . . . [T]his very problem was a chief cause of Our Father's [i.e., the devil] quarrel with the Enemy. When the creation of man was first mooted and when, even at that stage, the Enemy freely confessed that He foresaw a certain episode about a cross, Our Father very naturally sought an interview and asked for an explanation. The Enemy gave no reply except to produce the cock-and-bull story about disinterested love which He has been circulating ever since. This Our Father naturally could not accept. . . . We know that He cannot really love: nobody can: it doesn't make sense. If we could only find out what He is *really* up to![11]

We see here again that the devil cannot fathom the possibility of love; his assumption, of course, is that there must be some ulterior motive—because true love does not and cannot exist. And his lie to us is that God does not and cannot really love us.

For my part, this is the hardest part about the faith to believe—namely, *that God really loves us that much*. Far more difficult than the doctrine of the blessed Trinity, in my opinion, is the belief that the infinite and eternal God who created the universe cares so much about *me*, a humble speck of matter within the grand cosmos. But such—and no less—is the gospel.

God as Master vs. God as Father

As is hinted at in the opening chapters of Genesis, the devil seeks to portray God as *Master*, not a loving Father. Consider for a moment how much this changes the dynamic between us and God: if God is Master, his will and his law are arbitrary—that is, they may well have nothing to do with our good and our happiness; they are there just to keep us down—to keep us in check as creatures. Further, if God is Master and his will and his law are there only to

11. Lewis, *Screwtape Letters*, 100–101, emphasis original.

keep us in check, then it sets up a tension between our will and his will. In this dynamic, the fullest freedom we could attain can only come by way of divorcing ourselves from God and his law; God becomes the enemy of human freedom and fulfillment—human flourishing can only come about by freeing oneself *from* God.

But consider the reverse—God as Father: as Father, his will and his law are not arbitrary but are directed to our good and our happiness; like a good coach who may require certain things that are initially painful, there are always *reasons* for prescribing this or that action—and they are linked to our objective good and happiness. The fullest freedom attained here, moreover, would be to submit to the discipline of the coach, in order to attain the highest excellence possible. In this sense, God's moral laws make possible a *greater* freedom and a richer happiness than mere license ever could. In fact, as St. Paul teaches, license to sin only gives rise to "slavery"—for the power of sin is like an addiction.

Satan wants us to see God as Master; and it is in this sense that the Catechism of the Catholic Church describes sin as "*lack of trust.*"[12] That is, we're always looking for happiness, in everything we do; our desire for happiness underlies our deepest pursuits. When we sin, therefore, we lose trust that God's ways really are ordered to our happiness—we lose trust that God is our loving Father and see him only as master.

Consider for a moment: if you *knew* that your parents wanted nothing more than for you to be happy *and* if you were sure that they *knew* exactly what would make you happy, would you ever disobey? The answer is still probably "yes," but it would at least be irrational to do so.

The point is this: we sin because we think God is holding something back from us—he is holding some happiness back from us *for no good reason*, and so we grasp at the fruit. And in that moment, we have lost trust in God as Father and have come to see him more as an overbearing Master whose law is there only to keep us down. This is the devil's lie.

---

12. *Catechism of the Catholic Church*, no. 397.

How Much Does God Loves Us?

Consider the prodigal son in Luke 15. We often think of this as a great story of the repentance of the younger son, of someone who turned his life around. And it is that, to be sure; but the story is even more deeply about *the unconditional love of the father*. The father sees the son in the distance and puts aside all sense of cultural self-respect: he *runs* to meet the son in the distance, puts a ring on his finger and shoes on his feet—and throws a party to celebrate his return! The father is only concerned about the son's return and cares nothing for his own public disgrace.

My friends, *we are the one lost sheep* that the Son came to save. *We* are the pearl of great price in God's eyes! *We* are the one the Father runs to in the story. We have a God who is madly in love with each and every one of us. And he loves us just the way we are, but too much to leave us that way. We cannot even begin to comprehend our worth in God's eyes.

This is mystery of mysteries—but it is the gospel. And God sent his son to show us this love, to redeem us, and to infuse his own divine life into us—and thereby make us his children.

Consider for a moment that if your mechanic ripped you off, you would be upset; and if six months later he apologized, you might forgive him. But what if I told you that this happened to someone and not only did they forgive the mechanic, they invited him into their home; and not just for one evening as a guest, but they invited him into their home permanently; and not just to use the spare bedroom—rather, they adopted the mechanic into their home as a son and had his name written into their will so that he could inherit the estate right alongside their other children.

We would think this is crazy—a bit over the top, right? But such is the gospel. In fact, this analogy pales in comparison. The devil will seek to snatch this seed from our soul—that God really loves us *that* much. But this is the gospel; we must prayerfully nurture this seed, moving it from our head to our heart.

As we said earlier, this kind of confidence in God's abiding and steadfast love for each of us *individually* and *personally* is something the devil hates. If we know this truth, we are on a sure and steadfast path to sanctity—giving us a peace that the world, the flesh, and the devil cannot take away. As St. John says elsewhere, "See what love the Father has given us, that we should be called children of God, *and so we are*" (1 John 3:1).

Salvation is not just about avoiding hell; it's about becoming children of God—sharing in, by grace, what the Eternal Son has by nature. Moral perfection couldn't earn one ounce of this divine life. And as we get a glimpse of how much God has done for us, we start to realize that Christianity is about so much more than obeying a certain set of rules. Salvation is becoming a child of God, in and through Christ—and growing up and maturing as children of God. As we have said, a father loves his kids just the way they are, but too much to leave them that way. The same is true of God; and through the power of the Spirit, he wishes to transform us from the inside out—from fallen creatures into divine-like lovers.

In the next chapter, we will look more closely at the "gift" of our lives; that is, we will look at how the perspective of creation changes everything—how everything we are and everything we have is utter gift. Truly, our lives, our time, and our bodies are not our own—we have been bought with a price (1 Cor 6:20). And we are in turn called to make a gift of what we have so graciously received.

Chapter 11

Letter 21: Stewards, Not Owners

As we saw in the last chapter, our God is himself utter gift. And all that we are and all that we have is utter gift—this the clear truth of creation.

But in this letter, Screwtape seeks to inculcate in the patient a sense of *ownership*—ownership of his life and all that goes with it; that is, Screwtape wants the patient to forget the basic truth of creation, in order to exploit what happens to the man when his sense of ownership turns to disappointment—leading to anger and frustration. Screwtape writes:

> Men are not angered by mere misfortune, but misfortune conceived as injury. And the sense of injury depends on the feeling that a legitimate claim has been denied. *The more claims on life, therefore, that your patient can be induced to make, the more often he will feel injured and, as a result, ill-tempered.* Now you will have noticed that nothing throws him into a passion so easily as to find a tract of time which he reckoned on having at his own disposal unexpectedly taken from him. It is the unexpected visitor . . . that throw[s] him out of gear.[1]

What is interesting about this letter is that, as has so often been the case, Screwtape sees the truth very clearly—much more so than the patient. In reality, our lives are not our own; we are *stewards* of all that we have, *not owners*. And so Screwtape continues:

> The assumption which you want him to go on making is so absurd that, if once it is questioned, even we cannot find a shred of argument in its defense. The man

1. Lewis, *Screwtape Letters*, 111, emphasis added.

can neither make, nor retain, one moment of time; it all comes to him by pure gift; he might as well regard the sun and moon as his chattels.[2]

Screwtape's whole game is predicated upon the man viewing his life—and especially his time—as his own; and when charity requests his attention, he will resent it—precisely because he feels that something of *his* is being *taken*:

> They anger him because he regards his time as his own and feels that it is being stolen. You [Wormwood] must therefore zealously guard in his mind the curious assumption "My time is my own." Let him have the feeling that he starts each day as the lawful possessor of twenty-four hours. Let him feel as a grievous tax that portion of this property which he has to make over to his employers, and as a generous donation that further portion which he allows to religious duties. *But what he must never be permitted to doubt is that the total from which these deductions have been made was, in some mysterious sense, his own personal birthright.*[3]

Creation

But what if we began each day from the perspective of creation? That would mean that we're aware of the fact that all that we are and all that we have is utter *gift*.

It would mean that the environment around us is a gift from God—of which we are not *owners*, but *stewards*, caring for what is not in fact ours. In fact, it's precisely because we are unique amidst all of creation that we are responsible for it.[4]

It would mean that our time is not our own—as hard as this would be to come to grips with; it would mean that our lives are part of the great stream of gift flowing from God himself—given

2. Ibid., 112.

3. Ibid., emphasis added.

4. For more on this theme, see my article on Pope Francis's encyclical, entitled "Laudato Si, Creation & Humanism."

to us precisely so that we may play our own part in giving it away to others. So, when someone needs us, we should let the divine life surge through us—participating however we can in God's providence. There is always a story going on that is bigger than ourselves; and when we're attentive to the promptings of the Holy Spirit, we become part of the great tapestry and drama of God's saving work.

Thus, while planning appropriately for the future is still the duty of the present, we need to try to become a little less rigid with our plans. There's a saying that goes like this: *if you want to make God laugh, tell him your plans.* Yes, we should plan; but we also need to be swift to bend with the winds of divine providence and be instruments of *his* plan, not ours.

The perspective of creation also means that our bodies are not our own. The phrase "I can do what I like with my body" really doesn't mesh with creation—because it's not *my* body. In fact, Screwtape sees this quite clearly:

> Much of the modern resistance to chastity comes from men's belief that they "own" their bodies—those vast and perilous estates, pulsating with the energy that made the worlds, in which they find themselves without their consent and from which they are ejected at the pleasure of Another![5]

God sees and knows all; and he speaks to us every day, if only we have hearts attentive enough to hear his voice. Before we do anything with our bodies, we should ask: *Is this the way the Creator would like me to use my body? Am I doing so in accordance with the purpose for which it was made? Am I glorifying the image of God inscribed in my body?*

Our lives are not our own; we have been bought with a price, and our bodies have become temples of the living God, as St. Paul famously states:

> Do you not know that your body is a temple of the Holy Spirit within you, which you have from God? You are not

5. Ibid., 113.

your own; you were bought with a price. So glorify God
in your body. (1 Cor 6:19–20)

In Matthew 25, Jesus lays out a scene regarding the final judg-
ment, and his question to us is whether or not we "fed the hungry,"
"gave drink to the thirsty," etc. (Matt 25:31–40). In other words,
the question in effect is: *Did we think of our lives as our own, or did
we see our lives as a gift—a gift which was then to be given away to
others?* Jesus did not say, "Well, those who didn't do anything *really*
bad, come with me to heaven." Rather, he basically said, "*Did you
love me in the people around you—and did you go out of your way
to do so?*" For Screwtape, this is not a nice lofty teaching for the
elite—this is what is at stake for every single one of us:

> And all the time the joke is that the word "Mine" in its
> fully possessive sense cannot be uttered by a human be-
> ing about anything. In the long run either Our Father or
> the Enemy will say "Mine" of each thing that exists, and
> especially of each man. They will find out in the end, nev-
> er fear, to whom their time, their souls, and their bodies
> really belong—certainly not to *them*, whatever happens.
> At present the Enemy says "Mine" of everything on the
> pedantic, legalistic ground that He made it: Our Father
> hopes in the end to say "Mine" of all things on the more
> realistic and dynamic ground of conquest.[6]

Our lives are not our own. And as Screwtape recounts, that
will be made clear someday. Let's participate in the great dance of
creation and God's providence by playing our part and doing so
generously. We do that best precisely when we do not regard our
lives as our own; for it is much easier to be generous—with our
entire lives—when we realize that we are first recipients of God's
ineffable generosity. When we realize first what we've been *given*
and the mercy that's been bestowed upon us, then we are better
able to imitate that divine goodness for those around us.

Practically, as we've seen, we can do this by realizing that *our*
projects, tasks, and ambitions are not the most important things
in the universe; as we've seen, when we are less self-consumed

6. Ibid., 114–15, emphasis original.

and preoccupied, we are more free to love—we are more *available*, mentally and physically, to those around us.

Conversely, when we think of our lives as something that is *ours*, we are less inclined to give of ourselves; and when we do give of ourselves in this state of mind, we do so begrudgingly—feeling as if we are doing the other person a *favor*, which then places them in "debt" to us (i.e., now they "owe" us). Here, we are in effect "keeping score."

But what if our lives are not *ours* to begin with? Then we feel palpably the seeds of generosity grow up within us, and now we are ready to make a difference—a difference Jesus asks us all to make.

And the great gospel paradox is that true joy and true life is found only when we give our lives away; indeed, only in giving do we truly receive.

In the next chapter, we shift gears a bit, discussing matters concerning the "historical" Jesus. Many Christians have had their faith shaken by scholarly revisionist history purporting to have established who the "real" Jesus was. How do we reconcile the Christ of faith—the Jesus we know and love in devotion—with these historical studies?

We will offer guidance in dealing with these proposals, both historically and philosophically. We will also take up the perennial question Jesus poses to us all: "*Who do you say that I am?*" (Matt 16:15). That is, we will look briefly at Jesus' claims regarding his own divinity, especially when his statements are understood against the backdrop of his first-century Jewish context.

Chapter 12

Letter 23: Faith, Doubt, and the Historical Jesus

As we noted, this letter strikes a slightly different chord; but it is an issue that we must work through, for it can greatly impinge upon our ability to live the Christian life. If one begins to doubt the reality of Jesus historically, then the power of his presence in our lives today begins to lose its footing.

You may have seen on occasion provocative claims made about the "historical" Jesus, usually purporting to demonstrate why traditional beliefs are incorrect—often coming out in timely fashion around Easter each year. And you or people you know may well have been unnerved by what they saw or heard.

In this letter, Screwtape wants to encourage such studies. His reason is principally to distract us from the real living Jesus—that is, Screwtape's main goal is to destroy our devotion in the present.

History, as we'll see in a moment—especially ancient history—is something that's always taken to some extent on faith; it's about accepting the testimony of someone else, since we weren't there. That's the first reason why purported claims to have finally discovered *objectively* the historical Jesus are somewhat of a charade.

What Screwtape sees in this attempt to get *behind* the historical sources (since the sources have remained more or less constant for some two thousand years) is inevitably somewhat speculative—a bit of hypothetical card stacking, which is bound to distort the real Jesus; that is, such theories are bound to overemphasize some real point in the data, the exaggeration of which creates an alternative (and for Screwtape, *fictional*) Jesus.

The ironic result, as some have pointed out over the years, is that the "historical" Jesus often turns out to look a lot like the scholar propounding the theory. That is, all too often, Jesus is simply remade in this or that person's image—and then is often exploited to push this or that *contemporary* agenda.[1] In other words, very often such studies are every bit as much about the *present* as they are the *past*. Screwtape writes:

> The advantages of these constructions, which we intend to change every thirty years or so, are manifold. In the first place they all tend to direct men's devotion to something which does not exist, for each "historical Jesus" is unhistorical. The documents say what they say and cannot be added to; each new "historical Jesus" therefore has to be got out of them by suppression at one point and exaggeration at another and by that sort of guessing (*brilliant* is the adjective we teach humans to apply to it) on which no one would risk ten shillings in ordinary life, but which is enough to produce a crop of new Napoleons, new Shakespeares, and new Swifts, in every publisher's autumn list.[2]

Everyone seems to be interested in Jesus—and everyone wants to be able to show that Jesus is really on their side when it comes to some contemporary debate, regardless of the political spectrum.[3] Screwtape alludes to this point here, noting how the accent mark is ultimately placed *not on Jesus himself*, but on the theory he is supposed to have taught:

> In the second place, all such constructions place the importance of their historical Jesus in some peculiar theory He is supposed to have promulgated. . . . We thus distract men's minds from who He is, and what He did.[4]

---

1. See Jenkins, *Hidden Gospels*, 16.
2. Lewis, *Screwtape Letters*, 124, emphasis original.
3. Jenkins, *Hidden Gospels*, 16.
4. Ibid., 125.

Thus, Jesus becomes important because of some theory he supposedly espoused—the theory becoming the matter of prime importance, and Jesus merely a means to that end.

Further, Screwtape encourages these reconstructions of the "historical" Jesus because they tend to make it harder and harder for the person living today to relate to this Jesus; such studies tend to bury Jesus in the past, as a man who lived a long time ago, who remains perhaps for us a curiosity, but not someone we can encounter in the present—certainly not someone we can worship with devotion and who can make a difference in our lives today:

> Our third aim is, by these constructions, to destroy the devotional life. For the real presence of the Enemy, otherwise experienced by men in prayer and sacrament, we substitute a merely probable, remote, shadowy, and uncouth figure, one who spoke a strange language and died a long time ago. Such an object cannot in fact be worshipped.[5]

If anybody has ever introduced students to such historical studies, he or she knows this to be a true; either the movement described above occurs—where devotion starts to erode—or students resist such studies like the plague, probably in part because they sense this very tension.

So, how do we reconcile the Jesus we know and love with the Jesus of history? What questions should we be asking ourselves when it comes to such studies and methods? How do we respond and not fall into Screwtape's trap?

In what follows, we will offer philosophical and historical guidance that acknowledges such historical studies, but tries to contextualize them by asking the right questions and avoiding the snares laid out by Screwtape.

5. Ibid.

Philosophical Bias

Sometimes claims regarding the "historical" Jesus have a naturalistic philosophical bias driving their conclusions; for example, when one reads something like "such and such a Gospel *must* have been written after the fall of the temple because the text seems to 'know' that such an event has already occurred," we should see readily that this is a *philosophical* conclusion, not a historical one.[6] In other words, for example, the Gospels of Matthew and Luke are often said to be written after the destruction of the Temple in AD 70 precisely because of the accuracy of Jesus' prophecy concerning this event. Such a position is *assuming that true prophecy cannot occur*—a position that might make sense if God didn't exist, but one that is preposterous if he does.

There is often a similar bias against miracles. Sometimes writers will act as if some miracle "could not have occurred," and they will present this as a "historical" conclusion. But notice, it's really a philosophical worldview that is driving the historical conclusion—not historical evidence per se.[7]

Historical Method

In some ways the discipline of historical Jesus studies suffers from the legacy of Rene Descartes (1596–1650), who proposed methodic doubt as the guiding principle of all knowledge; that is, in his view, *what can be doubted must be doubted*.[8] Descartes wanted absolute certainty before he would assent to anything. The problem, of course, is that historical inquiry does not lend itself to such mathematical certainty.

In historical Jesus studies, one methodological principle that expresses this Cartesian doubt is the principle of "dissimilarity." This principle stipulates that if something Jesus said or did is

6. See Lewis, *Miracles*, 3.

7. See Keener, *Miracles*, 33–34, 107–70.

8. See *Discourse on Method*, part 4, in Descartes, *Discourse on Method and Meditations on First Philosophy*, 18.

dissimilar to what early Christians believed, then it can be trusted as historically accurate. Jesus' baptism is usually taken as an example that passes this test because it seems to make Jesus inferior to John the Baptist—contrary to early Christian belief.

Now, on the surface, such a procedure makes sense. But when the procedure is turned the other way around, it becomes problematic. That is, when Jesus says/does things that are *similar* to what the early Christians believed, these sayings/events are to be rejected as early church propaganda—writing their own beliefs onto the lips of Jesus. Such a procedure exhibits what is sometimes called a "hermeneutic of suspicion," i.e., assuming the text to be guilty until proven innocent.

This is dubious at a basic historical level: as renowned New Testament scholar N. T. Wright has pointed out, the real Jesus must be the historical bridge between Judaism and early Christianity;[9] in other words, why in the world would we ever assume that there should be *no continuity* between the founder (Jesus) and the movement (Christianity) he gave rise to?

Reasonable Belief

We should ask the historical question differently—not seeking absolute certainty, but seeking reasonable belief. After all, history—especially ancient history—is all about accepting someone else's testimony regarding happenings to which we were not privy. That is, certitude is simply not an appropriate standard for history; rather, history moves between levels of plausibility and probability—that is, reasonable belief.

Therefore, the question we should ask is whether the testimony of the Gospels makes sense within the context of first-century Judaism. For if there is anything on which virtually all contemporary historical Jesus scholars agree, it's that the historical Jesus must make sense in light of his first-century Jewish context.

9. Wright, *Jesus and the Victory of God*, 132, 226, 450.

So, when it comes to the Gospels, the question we should ask is whether there is the familiarity we would expect of an eyewitness, with regard to Palestinian geography, Jewish custom, culture, and the political situation on the ground. In other words, are the Gospels *consistent* with what we know about the period? And can the Jesus they portray account for the rise of Christianity? As Brant Pitre said quite well:

> If a saying or deed attributed to Jesus is contextually plausible, coherent with other evidence about Jesus, and ... provides a plausible cause for the practice and belief of the early church, then it is reasonable to conclude that the evidence in question is historical.[10]

So how do the Gospels fare? Well, contrary to the trend of the so-called "Gnostic Gospels," the canonical Gospels are quite at home with the geography of the Holy Land (e.g., Bethany, Capernaum, and the like are real cities that one can still visit to this day). They are familiar with Jewish customs and Jewish groups—and their various points of contention (e.g., Pharisees and Saduccees). Moreover, the canonical Gospels situate their accounts in the context of real rulers and figures that we know about from other historical sources: e.g., Caesar Augustus, Tiberius, Pontius Pilate, Quirinius, Festus, Felix, Herod the Great, Herod Antipas, Herod Agrippa, Annas, and Caiaphas.

In other words, everything about the Gospels has the feel of eyewitness testimony—of people on the ground at the actual time and having real knowledge of the actual political situation, culture, custom, and geography. The absence of such familiarity in the so-called "Gnostic Gospels" is what makes the vast majority of scholars date such works no earlier than the second half of the second century; whereas even the likes of Bart Erhman (an atheist/agnostic New Testament scholar) acknowledge that the canonical Gospels are first-century documents, and as such are our earliest sources for the life of Jesus. Erhman writes:

10. Pitre, *Jesus and the Last Supper*, 41.

As it turns out, the New Testament Gospels are our best sources. They are best not because they happen to be in the New Testament, but because they are also the earliest narratives of Jesus's life to survive.[11]

Putting It All Together

What we have in some ways is similar to arguments for God's existence; that is, we have an inference from a perceived effect to an unseen cause. Such a procedure is not foreign to the sciences either—after all, how do we know about quarks and other subatomic particles, or black holes? We know about such realities by inferring them from their effects.

The historical effect to be explained in our case is the rise of Christianity; if we simply compare Christianity with other Jewish messianic movements of the day (and there were several), the historically curious thing is that in every case, *when the leader died, the movement died*, with one exception—*Christianity*.[12] So, just at a historical level, something seems to be different about Christianity—and Jesus' resurrection has the power to account for this difference. Without the resurrection, it would seem that we have an effect (the rise of Christianity) with no adequate cause.

The fact is, a gentle/hippie Jesus who just told people to be nice and get along would never have gotten crucified; he would never have drawn the crowds that he did, and he would never have caught the attention of either the Jewish or Roman authorities.

But a Jesus who, as the new Moses, is bringing about the new exodus hoped for by the prophets—who is bringing about a new Passover and offers new manna and is himself the new and eschatological Temple—such a Jesus both makes sense coming out

---

11. Erhman, *How Jesus Became God*, 89–90.

12. Wright, *Resurrection of the Son of God*, 557–59, and Evans, *Jesus, the Final Days*, 91–95.

of Judaism and has the power to explain the rise of Christianity, particularly once his claims are vindicated by the resurrection.[13]

Dating the Gospels

By the end of Acts of the Apostles, Paul is still alive and is awaiting his trial in Rome. Paul was martyred under Emperor Nero in the mid-60s. And Acts is the sequel to the Gospel of Luke (cf. Luke 1:1–4; Acts 1:1–2). Since Acts covers Paul's missionary journeys, there is no reason why Luke (the author of Acts) would be silent about the climax of Paul's life and ministry, namely, his martyrdom—*unless such an event had not yet occurred.*[14] This strongly suggests that Acts was written *before* Paul's death in the mid-60s—and that suggests that the Gospel of Luke is even earlier still. This is significant because it places the written testimony of Jesus within the generation of living witnesses.

Writing to the Corinthians, St. Paul states that the risen Jesus appeared to over five hundred people at one time—*"most of whom are still alive"* (1 Cor 15:6). That is, the people to whom he is writing *knew the truth*—either from themselves or from living eyewitnesses.

Just imagine for a moment that someone wrote a book ten years from now about me and the miracles I performed while teaching at Benedictine College. Surely, people would soon give their counter-testimony against such an outrageous claim. *You simply can't fabricate grandiose narratives in the presence of living witnesses.* In fact, it's been suggested that the development of legendary materials takes at least three to four generations, precisely because living witnesses need to be gone before legendary materials can gain traction.[15]

We can be confident that the Gospels stem from eyewitness testimony and tell the truth about what Jesus said and did.

---

13. Pitre, *Jesus and the Jewish Roots of the Eucharist*, 22–47.

14. Pitre, *Case for Jesus*, 98–101.

15. Kreeft, *Handbook of Christian Apologetics*, 190–91.

Remember, the Gospels themselves *are* historical evidence—we shouldn't fall into the trap of thinking that evidence only counts when it's from a secular source.

As Screwtape himself acknowledges, the Gospels are the principle evidence for the life of Jesus; and they should be given the benefit of the doubt—especially since they are so clearly rooted in the real first-century Jewish setting in which Jesus lived.

And their portrait of Jesus has the power to explain the rise of Christianity, whereas alternative revisionist claims do not. In the words of Pope Emeritus Benedict:

> Unless there had been something extraordinary in what happened, unless the person and the words of Jesus radically surpassed the hopes and expectations of the time, there is no way to explain why he was crucified or why he made such an impact.[16]

Who Do You Say that I Am?

With this basic background of confidence regarding the historicity of the Gospels in mind, let's take a look at the next and most important question: namely, *who is Jesus?*

In the following, I will seek to show the union between the Christ of the creeds (the Christ of faith) and the Jesus of history; we will especially seek to show how Jesus described and taught his own divinity—coequal with the Father—but that he did so in a *Jewish* way; that is, in a way that makes sense in the context of first-century Judaism.

On the one hand, the Gospel of John is very clear regarding the divinity of Jesus (see John 1:1–4, 14; 5:17–18; 8:58–59 [compare with the Greek Old Testament Exod 3:14]; 10:30–33; 20:28 [compare with Rev 19:9–11]). On the other hand, since some claim Jesus' divinity is only taught in John's Gospel, we will focus our attention on other passages in the Synoptic Gospels (Matthew, Mark, and Luke), which—in their first-century Jewish

---

16. Benedict XVI, *Jesus of Nazareth*, xxii.

context—are no less clear regarding the divinity of Jesus. Finally, we will also take a look at one passage from St. Paul. The key, again, for these Synoptic passages is that Jesus reveals his divinity, but in a distinctively Jewish way.

The Temple

In Matthew 12:6, Jesus says of himself, "something greater than the temple is here" (see also John 2:19–21). To the ancient Jew, the temple was the very dwelling place of God (see 1 Kgs 8:10; Exod 40:35). *In first-century Judaism, the only thing that could possibly be greater than the temple would be God himself!* This is a mighty claim when understood in its first-century Jewish setting.

The Sabbath

Further, in Matthew 12 Jesus describes himself as "lord of the Sabbath" (Matt 12:8); God's rest on the seventh day (Gen 2:2–3) is the foundation of the Sabbath. Again, who could be *lord* of the Sabbath, except God himself?

The Law

In the Sermon on the Mount, Jesus places his own teaching on the same level as the Torah—which to an ancient Jew, was the very revelation of God. Jesus gives six "antitheses" where he says, "You have heard that it was said . . . *But I say to you*" (Matt 5:21, 27, 31, 33, 38, 43), supplementing and enhancing the Law, as for example here: "You have heard that it was said, 'You shall not commit adultery'. *But I say to you* that everyone who looks at a woman lustfully has already committed adultery with her in his heart" (Matt 5:28). Accordingly, the crowds were "astonished" because Jesus taught them "as one who had authority, and not as their scribes" (Matt 7:28). Usually, the scribes would attempt to *explain* God's revelation; but Jesus' teaching *is* revelation. That is, *Jesus' teaching is a new font of revelation on par with the Torah*—something which no mere Jewish teacher or scribe could possibly say of their own teaching in the first century.

The Rich Young Man

In the scene with the rich young who asks Jesus how to inherit eternal life, we have another implicit divine claim—although it does not seem so at first glance. Jesus perhaps shockingly responds to the young man's initial question by saying, "Why do you call me good? No one is good but God alone" (literally: "except for the one God") (Mark 10:18). As is well known, Jesus responds by going through the commandments ("Do not kill . . . steal . . . commit . . . adultery . . ."). The young man responds by noting that he has kept these from his youth (v. 20). Now, lest we look upon the young man as deceitful and arrogant, let's notice how Jesus responds: "And Jesus looking upon him *loved him* . . ." That is, Jesus doesn't seem to dispute the young man's conscience—yet, one thing remains.

By the end, Jesus famously says: "You lack one thing; go sell what you have . . . *and come follow me*" (v. 21). Jesus' final statement here can only make sense if Jesus is in fact God in the flesh: for here Jesus attaches salvation not just to the commandments, *but to following him*. In other words, there is no way a mere ancient Jewish teacher could say that following *him* is essential to salvation—in *addition* to keeping Torah. But, as with the above in the Sermon on the Mount—where Jesus' teaching is placed on par with (and even supplementing) the Torah—here following Jesus is said to be every bit as essential (in fact, more so) to salvation as keeping the Law. Such a statement, in the context of first-century Judaism, makes no sense unless Jesus is implicitly pointing to his own divinity—equal to the God of Israel. And that's exactly what Jesus is claiming: because of *who* he is, the commandments alone are not enough; they must be supplemented by attaching oneself firmly and directly to Jesus.

It is because of statements like these that contemporary Jewish rabbi and scholar Jacob Neusner concludes: "I now realize, only God can demand of me what Jesus is asking."[17]

Forgiving Sins

The way in which Jesus offered forgiveness of sin—*through himself*—left no doubt in the minds of his hearers that he was assuming the prerogatives of God. In Mark 2:5, Jesus heals a paralytic and says, "Child, your sins are forgiven." Immediately, the scribes witnessing the event express their disgust: "Why does this man speak like this. It is blasphemy! *Who can forgive sins but God alone?*" (Mark 2:7). Again, Jesus' actions in context leave the unmistakable impression that he is claiming to be God in the flesh.

Just Passing By

In Mark's Gospel, when Jesus walks on water the text curiously describes him as intending to "*pass by*" the apostles (Mark 6:48–49). It's a strange phrase—where could he be going?

This cryptic reference is an allusion to Old Testament scenes where YHWH appeared and "*passed by*." Consider these two episodes with Moses and Elijah: "[The Lord said to Moses], 'I will make my goodness *pass before you*. . . . While my glory *passes by* . . . I will cover you . . . until I have *passed by*'. . . . The Lord *passed before* him" (Exod 33:19, 22; 34:6); and with Elijah: "And behold, the Lord *passed by*" (1 Kgs 19:11). Both the Septuagint (the Greek Old Testament) in these passages and Mark's Gospel use the verb *parerchomai* to describe this "*passing by*" of the Lord. The point is clear: *when Jesus walks on water and "passes by" the apostles, the text is showing us that he is the God of Israel come in the flesh.*[18]

---

17. Neusner, *Rabbi Talks with Jesus*, 68, cited in Benedict XVI, *Jesus of Nazareth*, 115.

18. Pitre, *Case for Jesus*, 129–30.

Every Knee Shall Bend

In Philippians 2:6–11, St. Paul describes Jesus' self-emptying and suffering unto death, which then leads to his exaltation. At the conclusion of this passage, we read: "Therefore . . . at the name of Jesus, every knee should bow . . . and every tongue confess that Jesus Christ is Lord" (Phil 2:9–11). This passage is well known, but what is often missed is how St. Paul is appropriating to Jesus *exactly what was said of YHWH* in the Old Testament: "To me [YHWH] *every knee shall bow*, every *tongue* shall swear" (Isa 45:23). In effect, Paul is saying that YHWH has become incarnate in and through Jesus—that Jesus is equal to YHWH!

A Final Thought

History is important because God became man in time and space. This has always been one of the most attractive aspects of Christianity: namely, that it's not merely a philosophy or a religious meditation; rather, Christianity is based upon real events—things that really happened in space and time—in the midst of real history, where people saw and touched the real Jesus.

After all, compare this to other ancient myths—where are the missionaries of Zeus or Osiris? There are no missionaries because mythic religion is fundamentally different than Christianity. Christianity had missionaries from the very beginning because these things took place in real space and time. That's why early Christians went to the ends of the known world—because they encountered something tangible and real. The same cannot be said for other mythic figures who didn't reside in a specific, concrete point in time and history. By comparison, this *historical* character is something unique to the Judeo-Christian tradition.

But though Jesus sanctified time and history by entering it, he still remains transcendent. This is on full display in his resurrection and ascension: the risen Jesus is no longer bound by time and space—and that's why he lives to encounter us in the ever present.

I tried to drive this point home to a group of students when we all went on a pilgrimage to the Holy Land in Israel. As we were leaving I said, "This has been amazing—to walk in the very footsteps of Jesus. But this is where Jesus *was*. The Eucharist is where Jesus *is*."

The point is that Jesus *lives* and he wishes to encounter us each and every day. His presence is no longer confined to a plot of land or limited to a specific point in time and history, as it was before his resurrection and ascension. Now, as Jesus says very clearly, "wherever two or three are gathered in my name, there I am in their midst" (Matt 18:20).

This is why, if we are going to encounter the real Jesus, we need both faith and reason—we need both historical context *and* devotion. In doing so, we encounter the *real* living Jesus, both in his humanity and divinity.

We don't say, "Jesus *was*," but that "Jesus *is*"—because he lives; Jesus conquered death because he is the God-man; Jesus remains present with us because he is God. This is the Jesus that Screwtape does *not* want us to encounter.

In the next chapter, we turn once again to prayer, but here with an eye toward the psychological tricks we sometimes play on ourselves. Screwtape makes much of this, in an attempt to discredit the power of prayer in our minds. We also take up the discussion of faith and reason, as it pertains to prayer: how do we understand our interaction with the infinite and eternal God—who already knows all? Does our prayer really *do* anything?

Chapter 13

Letter 27: Prayer and Reason

IN THIS LETTER, SCREWTAPE discusses the "haunting suspicion" that prayer does not work. We've all had the experience of praying for something that didn't quite turn out the way we wanted. This is of course the normal experience of every Christian from time to time.

What we're interested in here is the psychological tricks we sometimes play on ourselves which inadvertently stack the deck against God and against the reality of meaningful prayer—and thereby bring us to despair.

On the one hand, if we grant that God's ways are not our ways, then we should not be surprised that God doesn't immediately give us everything we want—especially at the time that we want it and in the way we want. And perhaps if we had God's vantage point, we might even see that his ways are better than ours—that perhaps, mysteriously, what we so earnestly prayed for would not have been for our good in the long run.

At the same time, Screwtape recounts the way in which we can more or less convince ourselves that prayer does not really work—how it can have no objective result:

> You [Wormwood] can worry him with the haunting sus-
> picion that the practice [i.e., prayer] is absurd and can
> have no objective result. Don't forget to use the "heads
> I win, tails you lose" argument. If the thing he prays for
> doesn't happen, then that is one more proof that peti-
> tionary prayers don't work; *if it does happen, he will, of*
> *course, be able to see some of the physical causes which led*
> *up to it, and "therefore it would have happened anyway,"*

> and thus a granted prayer becomes just as good a proof
> as a denied one that prayers are ineffective.[1]

This is so easy to fall into: we pray for something and it comes to pass, and then we subtly say to ourselves, "It would have happened anyway." Or, if it doesn't happen, we say, "See, prayer doesn't really do anything." Either way, God loses—the deck has already been stacked against the power of prayer.

In other words, these psychological traps don't really give God a fair shake—how could God possibly win here? No matter what, we have an explanation ready at hand which finds a way to exclude God.

What I've found is that there's always a way to exclude God if we really want to; if we don't want to believe, we don't have to. Remember what Screwtape said earlier: God won't use the "*irresistible*" or the "*indisputable.*" These matters aren't math problems—that is, God won't force our hand; if we want to find a way out without God, we'll find one.

But conversely, if we choose to see things in light of faith, we can always do that as well. We can turn from a cynical attitude to a faith-filled one, which first of all sees the natural order as part of God's providence. That is, *just because there are natural explanations and causes at work does not mean that God is uninvolved.* The cynical view is a false choice and prejudices things against God. Why couldn't God choose to work through these natural causes, as he so often does? Didn't he create nature?

Sometimes, God answers prayers through natural means and sometimes he speaks to us directly through the people around us; but if we are to receive these graces, we must first be open to the fact that he can do this.

Patience and Perseverance

We must be patient with God and we must trust his loving care, even if we don't feel like it. Recall our discussion earlier regarding

1. Lewis, *Screwtape Letters*, 148, emphasis added.

discernment: sometimes there is immense growth in the *process* of discernment itself—growth that would be cut short if we received an unmistakably clear answer right away. The same is true in prayer, because prayer—especially when we persevere—*changes us*. It's not just about getting what we want; it's also about becoming the kind of person that God wants us to become. We have to be open to the fact that he speaks to us on sunny days, but very often we are most sculpted by the divine chisel of hardship—and the patience and perseverance demanded of us in such situations.

It helps here to look back on a past time where we really grew through trial, but certainly didn't feel like it at the time. In the midst of hardship, we just want out of it; but if we reflect back on *past growth* through hardship, it can give us confidence that the current crisis will likewise yield positive fruit.

Similarly, we can look back at past times when we really prayed for something that didn't come to fruition, but where we still persevered in prayer; often when we look back, we can see the spiritual growth that took place precisely because we continued to pray. In fact, the transformation wrought in us was perhaps even more important (at least, in God's eyes) than the thing for which we prayed. And as we said, sometimes God even gives us a later glimpse that what we prayed for was actually not in our best interests—even though we couldn't see it at the time. As we look back and recognize these things (either our own past spiritual growth through trial, or God's wisdom in a prayer not granted), it helps us grow in faith and confidence. We grow in confidence that our prayers amidst the present trial really are making a difference, *in some way*, even though we may not be able to see it clearly right now.

Prayer and Reason

In this letter, Screwtape also raises the issues of time, freedom, and predestination—and the conundrums these mysteries can stir up for us, especially with regard to our prayer. People who have delved heavily into philosophy and metaphysics often speak of

God's inability to change, his immutability: change implies some acquisition of what was previously lacking; but if God is perfect how can he change? And if God can't change, what does that do to prayer? Does my prayer even matter, if God already knows what I'm going to say ahead of time?

These are good questions; but my answer is relatively simple. Metaphysics is wonderful and I believe Aristotle—and especially St. Thomas Aquinas—distilled some amazing truths; they show us what natural reason can do. But they also show us natural reason's limitations. For my part, the conundrums mentioned above are due to privileging Aristotle and metaphysics over the gospel. In truth, Aristotelian metaphysics, sublime as it is, must bend the knee to the revelation of Jesus Christ.

Aristotle came to the conclusion of monotheism; he knew that contemplating this one God was somehow man's ultimate end. But he didn't have a notion of a *personal* God who *loves* us. That wouldn't have made sense to him. And let's be honest: in terms of natural reason, how could it have? Why would the creator of the universe be so interested in *me* personally?

But as we've seen, that's the gospel! The Eternal Son became man in Jesus Christ not simply to teach us a few moral truths we had somehow forgotten, or to confirm that Aristotle's monotheism was basically right. Rather, Christ brought something *new*; and part of that novelty is the radical love of God for each of us *individually*—that this God seeks us each and every day—indeed, that he *"thirsts"* for us.

Jesus taught us to pray without ceasing—to "knock and the door shall be opened" (Matt 7:7). Jesus gives *no* indication that prayer is somehow a waste of time because metaphysically God knows everything already ahead of time. In, fact, *he's* the one who tells us that the Father knows what we need before we even ask (Matt 6:8). And yet *he* exhorts us to pray without ceasing, to be like the persistent widow with the unrighteous judge (Luke 18:1–8).

As Christian thinkers, we can cherish the truths of Aristotle, but we must filter them through the gospel. And here, we must feel free to part ways with the pagan thinker, great as he was.

Jesus teaches us over and over again that our faith needs to be like that of children (Matt 18:1–4). We can acknowledge that there are great mysteries involved concerning the way in which the eternal God interacts with us in time—how the Infinite interacts with the finite—but we can't allow one truth to trump another. That is, on the one hand, God *is* radically different from anything in the universe—and to this extent, Aristotelian metaphysics is right; still, on the other hand, Jesus teaches us very clearly regarding the efficacy and power of prayer. In our case, we can't allow the philosophical truth of Aristotle to trump what Jesus so clearly teaches. Both are true in some respect, but their perfect reconciliation is beyond our vantage point. While we assume that all truth can be reconciled in God's wisdom, we also recognize that our limited perspective will not be able to see how all the parts fit together in the whole of God's providence.

We must persevere in prayer and we must believe in its power. This is a test of faith; for praying is something that quite simply makes no sense—*unless one believes*; for the act of prayer is itself a great act of faith. When we pray, and when we persevere in prayer, our faith grows tremendously.

And when we stop praying, our faith tends to wither away and dry up. This may happen gradually; we may still read lots of books *about* God, think *about* God, and talk *about* God—even professionally. But if we don't talk *to* God, we're simply an outsider looking in. And the more we talk about God from the outside, the more we talk as an unbeliever. I say this not to sound harsh, but to note how easily and gradually this can happen. A few weeks like this can pass into months, and before one knows it, years go by without speaking intimately *with* God. And then we look up and wonder how in the world we got to where we are—we think back to a time when we really *knew* God. But now we have no idea how to retrace our steps—no way to get back to where we were—because so much has changed.

Our faith is the most prized possession we have; if we really cherish it, we must nurture it. And the best way to do that is to pray; if we don't practice our faith, we'll lose it. Prayer is a great act of faith and a "yes" to God. It says "I believe"—with one's whole heart and mind—far more loudly than we could ever say with mere words. This means something not only to God, but also to ourselves and our own growth. For as we have said, *prayer changes us*—and this is part of the process God so desires for us. It's not just about getting what we want, but allowing God to transform our hearts.

In the next and final chapter, we take up C. S. Lewis's famous line that "courage is the form" of every virtue. In this letter and our discussion of it, we will treat the centrality of courage, the true and abiding freedom of virtue, and the mystery of human suffering. Here, most assuredly, we find the seeds of true life.

Chapter 14

Letter 29: Courage and Suffering

IN THIS LETTER, SCREWTAPE reveals something special about courage, referring to it as the "form" of every virtue. His point here is that *without* courage, none of the other virtues can take shape; and even the very practice of the other virtues presupposes the virtue of courage. Screwtape writes:

> This, indeed, is probably one of the Enemy's motives for creating a dangerous world—a world in which moral issues come to the point. He sees as well as you [Wormwood] do that courage is not simply *one* of the virtues, but the form of every virtue at the testing point, which means at the point of highest reality. A chastity or honesty, or mercy, which yields to danger will be chaste or honest or merciful only on conditions. *Pilate was merciful till it became risky.*[1]

The Virtuous Circle

Classically, there are four virtues that have been referred to as the "cardinal" virtues—"cardinal" here coming from a Latin word meaning "hinge": these are the virtues upon which human life hinges.

Prudence is the first cardinal virtue and has been called the "charioteer" of the virtues because it has the task of directing the others. This virtue enables us to make sound moral decisions; it begins in the intellect and then leads to action.[2]

---

1. Lewis, Screwtape Letters, 161–62, emphasis added.
2. For a fuller discussion of these virtues, see my *John Paul II to Aristotle*

Justice is the virtue that enables us to give our neighbor his or her due; it is inherently relational and calls us to seek the natural good, honor, and respect due to others.

Courage is the virtue that enables us to face difficulties; it concerns both our inward emotional states and how these inward states aid or hinder our ability to be bold and daring when the circumstances call for it.

Temperance is the virtue that moderates our desire for bodily pleasure—for food, drink, and sex; like courage, it concerns both our inward emotional states and how these inward states aid or hinder our ability to temper our passions and desires.

So what is the virtuous circle? As mentioned above, prudence has been called the "charioteer" of the virtues; and since this virtue begins in the intellect, it has to lead the other virtues. After all, how can I be courageous unless I first identify (with prudence) what the courageous act looks like in this or that circumstance?

But on the other hand, if my internal passions and emotions are all over the place, how likely is it that I will be able to execute sober decisions? And so here we come to the virtuous circle: on the one hand, prudence must lead because the intellect must go first; on the other hand, I will have great difficulty exercising prudence if I do not *first* have temperance and courage—for if my passions and emotions are all over the place, it will be very difficult to make sound decisions. This is the circle: in one respect, prudence must lead; in another respect, courage and temperance are prerequisites to prudence—for the lack of these virtues dramatically hinders my ability to be prudent.

This is Screwtape's point—"Pilate was merciful *till it became risky.*" It's one thing to *know* what the right thing to do is; *it's another thing to do it.* Without courage, prudence will never get past merely *knowing* what one should do; courage is required to bring this knowledge to execution. And so to Screwtape's point: without courage, all of our virtues will be virtues *only to a point.* When we face resistance, if we don't have courage, we will crumble. In this sense, all of our virtues will go only as far as our courage will take them.

---

and Back Again, 23–38.

The Freedom of Virtue

In order to understand the virtue tradition more fully, all we need to do is translate what we know so well from other areas of life. In other words, in many areas, we know there is a deeper freedom than merely to choose to do what we want—a deeper freedom that is only attained through discipline. Consider the following examples:

- Learning a musical instrument
- Getting in shape
- Learning a foreign language
- Mastering any athletic skill or technique (e.g., a golf swing, pitching mechanics, shooting or dribbling a basketball)

In each of these endeavors, the early going is tough; it's awkward and clumsy at first. But as time goes on—if one perseveres—it gets easier and easier. As time goes by, one can for example run longer and harder than they ever could at the beginning. And here we see that it's not just external actions that are changing: the person is becoming different on the *inside*—they are *able* to do more and to do it more *consistently*, and with more *joy* than ever before.[3]

One attains these skills inwardly only by practicing them outwardly: by practicing the golf swing, for example, the correct way over and over, it becomes internalized; after a while, one does not have to think about it as much—it becomes "second nature." And that's when one starts to really become a good golfer. Before that, anybody can hit a lucky shot; but the good golfer is *reliable* and *consistent* because they have internalized the skill—it has become a part of them and will remain so as long as they continue to practice.

So too with virtue: by performing courageous acts externally, these acts over time change us on the inside. The more we *practice* courage in the little things, the easier it becomes the next time. The

3. For more on these themes, see my *John Paul II to Aristotle and Back Again*, 23–31.

same is true for all the virtues: like acts become like habits. We are *becoming* something new on the inside; as our character becomes more and more fixed through habit, we become more and more *reliable* and *consistent* in our ability to be the people we really want to be. In this sense, the moral question we should ask ourselves is not, "What do I do in this or that situation?" but, "*Who do I want to be?*"

As we practice such virtuous acts over the long haul, we develop a greater freedom to be a better person—and to do so *consistently*, *promptly*, and with *joy*. This gives us an ever-increasing freedom to love—the freedom to make our lives not about ourselves, but about others. And here, we begin to attain the freedom to be truly happy.

Mystery of Suffering

In our experience, I think we can identify the fear of suffering as lying behind those times when we fail to act as we should. Either I am afraid to go through the suffering (whether mental or physical) of confronting some evil, or I am afraid to undergo the pain of abstaining from something I want to do.

In this sense, courage can be seen as the ability *to do what I don't want to do*, and temperance as the ability *not to do what I want to do*.

And perhaps in this light, we see something of the divine wisdom and plan in the suffering of Christ and in our own suffering. Christ shows us radical love and radical courage in and through his self-offering on the cross. And if fear of suffering strikes at the heart of why we fail to live up to God's call for our lives, it is fitting that God would often use our trials to sculpt us into his masterpieces.[4] As much as we hate to admit it, we only really find out what we're made of through trial—and only through trial are we really transformed into all that we can really become. Just ask any athlete: it's through testing that one pushes through to the next level.

4. See Hahn, *Father Who Keeps His Promises*, 69, 73–76.

Further, in light of faith, we know that the deepest mystery of suffering is that the image of Christ crucified is being reproduced in and through us, as St. Paul says: "Now I rejoice in my sufferings for your sake *and in my flesh I complete what is lacking in Christ's afflictions* for the sake of his body, that is, the church" (Col 1:24). Now, strictly speaking, we know there is nothing lacking in Christ's afflictions; but what remains is for the paschal mystery— the suffering, death, and resurrection of Jesus—to be recapitulated or reproduced in and through each and every Christian.[5] What happened to Christ the head will be recapitulated in his body, the church; for this reason, Paul sees his own suffering as participating in this great process, through the power of the Spirit.

Thus, there is no Easter Sunday without Good Friday; this was true for Christ, and it remains true for us. In a mysterious way, our own suffering participates in his passion because the crucified Christ is being recapitulated in his mystical body. Remember what Jesus said to Saul (later St. Paul): "Saul, Saul, why do you persecute *me?*" (Acts 9:4). Not "my church" or "my followers"—but why do you persecute *me*. This shows us how tightly Jesus identifies with his followers—as St. Paul later said, "It is not I who live but Christ who lives in me" (Gal 2:20).

Suffering doesn't feel good, but sometimes it really makes us grow—something we usually only see in hindsight. But even more than that, suffering can be a powerful prayer when offered to God and placed at the foot of the cross; and it can become a powerful means through which we intimately participate in Christ's passion and allow his life to be reproduced in us. In a real sense, this is what Christianity is all about: for the Holy Spirit to reproduce the life, death, and resurrection of Jesus Christ in and through each of us; to make us fallen human beings into infinite divine lovers— who love like Christ until it hurts and beyond. This is the power

5. For St. Paul, this begins in baptism and is continued throughout our lives through the power of the Holy Spirit: "Do you not know that all of us who have been baptized into Christ Jesus were baptized into his death? We were buried therefore with him by baptism into death, so that as Christ was raised from the dead by the glory of the Father, we too might walk in newness of life" (Rom 6:3-4; see also Col 2:12).

of grace and the power of the Spirit. We must say with John the Baptist, "He must increase [and] I must decrease" (John 3:30), so that his risen life may flow in and through us.

Now we're almost to the end of our road. In a closing note, I offer you my parting thoughts. In truth, we are only at the beginning of the journey, not the end. For salvation history—for each of us individually and for the whole world—is always ongoing at each and every moment.

A Closing Note

THROUGH THE UNWITTING GUIDE of Screwtape, we have been on quite a journey. From domestic hatred, despair, evangelization, sarcasm, humility-as-self-forgetfulness, anxiety, the mystery of love, creation, the historical Jesus, prayer, suffering, and the centrality of courage—we have run the gamut of the human experience. We have traced the ways in which the devil seeks to dismantle our peace and joy, trying to get us to do and become "neither what we ought, nor what we like."

In untangling Screwtape's counsel, we have staked out a plan for spiritual survival in the twenty-first century—one built on turning outward in love of God and neighbor and thinking less about ourselves. Fueled by prayer and simply being ourselves, we can become the people we truly long to be; and in doing so we can gradually spread the peace and joy of knowing Christ to those around us.

In a real sense, conversion never stops, and that's why the spiritual battle for our souls is always on-going. And as we have seen, the little things *matter*—often much more than we realize.

There are a few aspects of the patient's life that I have left out—especially how his story ends and whether or not he makes it to heaven. Hopefully, this book has been a way for you to unpack the depths of what Lewis has to offer. But I didn't want to keep you from the real thing—so you'll have to turn to Lewis's own text to find out about the patient's ultimate destiny.

In the last part of this book, I have also included an appendix that summarizes St. Ignatius of Loyola's teaching on how to overcome spiritual desolation. Some of his thought has already made its way into this book, especially chapter 2, where we discussed the way in which Screwtape seeks to "exploit the tough period"—that is, the way in which the Evil One seeks to bring us to despair by exploiting our low spiritual moments. Many of my students have found great hope and inspiration in this teaching from Ignatius; indeed, his teaching here has the power to substantially remove the force of the devil's attacks—it has the power to set captives free.

Hopefully, you'll find the summary a quick and easy way to grasp the key concepts and see the power they have for helping us persevere through the ebb and flow of life—especially to get us through our spiritually dark moments. If we can get through these—and if we can get better at getting through these—then the devil will not be able to hold us down. Such is the force of Ignatius's teaching.

As I said at the opening, we're in this together—for no one is ever beyond the reach of Screwtape's tactics; nor is anyone ever beyond the reach of God's mercy. Rest assured, you will most certainly remain in my prayers.

In Christ Jesus our Lord,

Dr. Andrew Swafford

Appendix

Setting Captives Free: St. Ignatius on Overcoming Desolation

ST. IGNATIUS OF LOYOLA's teaching on how to overcome desolation is exceedingly practical. In this teaching, as I said, a great many of my students have found tremendous inspiration and hope; it has given them tools to get through the spiritual trials that every Christian faces—tools that help to fend off the despair in which the Evil One so desperately tries to ensnare us.

St. Ignatius's text is divided up into fourteen "rules" and I will organize my summary accordingly.[1]

First, a word on *desolation* and *consolation*: for Ignatius, "consolation" refers to any uplifting spiritual movement, a felt increase of faith and closeness to God. "Desolation" refers to the opposite, a sense of discouragement, doubt, despair, and a general feeling of God's distance or even absence.

Consolation and desolation are the normal ebb and flow of the Christian life; these periods can be long or short (perhaps alternating back and forth even within the same day), and they can each be of greater or lesser intensity.

For Ignatius, *consolation is from God* and *desolation is from the Evil One.* God *gives* consolation and he *allows* desolation. Nonetheless, both fall within the scope of God's providence; that is, God is ultimately at work in both. This foundational material concerning consolation and desolation covers the introductory content of rules 1–4.

---

1. My first encounter with Ignatius came through Fr. Timothy Gallagher's book *Discernment of Spirits*. My summary here is very much influenced by his presentation.

Rule 5 stipulates that *in desolation, never make a change.* That is, Ignatius counsels us to stick firmly to the spiritual resolutions we made while in consolation. The reason is that desolation is the time of the "lie"—it is not the time of sober thinking. It is the time of the Evil One's deception.

This pertains to big and small matters. For example, suppose I wake up one morning thinking, "I know I had planned on praying with my Bible for fifteen minutes every morning, but today I'm feeling down, so I won't pray at all." What often happens is that if the person sticks to their initial prayer resolutions, the downward spiritual pull may subside—they may again feel God's presence. But if, in their downward state, they give in and change their prior resolutions, it's likely that their desolation will only get worse.

This could also pertain to a vocational decision: the devil will try to get us to second-guess ourselves after we've committed in some way—especially when we're feeling down in desolation. For Ignatius, again, *when in desolation, never make a change.* Desolation is the time of the "lie," a time when we are more prone to the Enemy's deception. For Ignatius, we should stick to our original resolution—big or small.[2]

Rule 6 gives guidance regarding what to do while in desolation. Basically, we want to act intensely *against* the desolation itself. Ignatius recommends four things: prayer of petition, meditation, examination, and a suitable penance. We will treat the first two here.

Prayer of petition is simply asking God to help us through the desolation. Remember, desolation is a time when God feels distant, even absent—a time in which one is not inclined to pray at all. The act of praying itself here already works against the gravitational pull of desolation.

Secondly, meditation is especially helpful for the following reasons. The experience of desolation attempts to redefine our

2. Fr. Gallagher does distinguish between "spiritual" and "non-spiritual" desolation (e.g., psychological or even physiological). Ignatius's rules pertain only to *spiritual* desolation. One often *should* change things affecting psychological or physiological (i.e., non-spiritual) desolation. See Gallagher, *Discernment of Spirits*, 75.

spiritual past and purports to claim tyranny over our future. We are down and feel far from God, and in this state *we begin to doubt the reality of our past encounter with God, thinking that perhaps it was all in our minds.* Here at this point, we are viewing our past spiritual history through a distorted lens—that of our present desolation. And further, the experience of desolation makes us think that *it will always be like this in the future.*

Meditation works to counter both of these movements. Ignatius counsels meditating on God's loving care for us; this may be done in a general way, say, meditating on Psalm 23 ("The Lord is my shepherd . . ."); but even more practical, he recommends meditating on God's loving faithfulness for me *personally* in the past. Since desolation makes us *forget* these past encounters, the very act of meditating upon how God has been faithful to me personally in the past directly counters this movement of desolation; that is, it directly confronts desolation's spiritual tyranny over our past by contradicting its insinuation that we never really were close to God. By actively meditating upon a past difficult time where God brought us through, we begin to stir hope that he will do the same again in the present; in this very movement of our thoughts, the chains of despair and desolation are beginning to break.

Rule 7 pertains to our *thinking* in time of desolation; Ignatius counsels us here to choose to think of desolation as a trial permitted by God. This casts even the experience of desolation in the light of faith. A major aspect of the suffering of desolation is our sense of its meaninglessness and hopelessness. Seeing desolation as a trial permitted by God in light of faith already gives it meaning and thereby begins to give us hope.

A couple of things are happening here: as we learn to employ Ignatius's steps in the midst of desolation, we are learning to rise above our spontaneous emotional reactions in the moment and take active steps to resist desolation, whereas if we simply allow our spontaneous emotional reactions to dominate, then the experience of desolation only gets worse and more severe. In resisting desolation, we eventually come out of desolation. Further, by getting better at resisting, we are more prepared to resist desolation in the future. This is in part why God allows desolation: *in resisting, we get better at resisting—and thus the shackles of desolation begin to lose their grip on us and the captives are being set free.*

Rule 8 gives us a glimpse of Ignatius's spiritual boldness; his counsel here is that when in desolation, one should *think that consolation will return soon.* Again, this is exactly contrary to the movement of desolation: the unbearable grip of desolation, as we have said, is precisely the sense that *it will last forever.* Here, rule 8 directly counters this by asking us to choose to believe that consolation will return *soon.* The very act of thinking that consolation will soon return stirs hope—once again directly undermining the downward pull of desolation. As hope grows, the desolation itself begins to wane and gives way to consolation.

Rule 9 offers three reasons for why God allows desolation, one of which we have already hinted at above. The first reason is that perhaps we have been spiritually negligent in some area; in other words, while our life may be moving in general toward the Lord, perhaps in some area we have regressed a bit. Here, the desolation may serve as a call to conversion, a "wake-up call" of sorts.

The second of God's reasons is simply to teach us some spiritual lesson—for us to grow in some way, perhaps in learning to overcome desolation more effectively and consistently.

The third reason is to show us our absolute dependence upon God. In consolation, we are often inflated with pride, thinking that we can take on the world. In desolation, we really come face to face with our lowliness, in which case, we can better see our radical need for grace.

Practically, if we are undergoing desolation, we should first ask ourselves if it could be due to the first reason: have we been negligent in some area of our spiritual life? If not, then we should rest assured that God has in mind reasons two or three. At that point, we should quietly embrace whatever it is that God wants us to learn in the midst of desolation.

As we have said, simply having this perspective of faith in mind in the midst of desolation directly undermines the strength of desolation and is a huge step toward moving out of it.

In sum, rules 5–9 are basically about what to do while in a state of desolation: rule 5, don't make a spiritual change; rule 6, *do* actively resist desolation by prayer and meditation; rule 7, choose to think of desolation in light of faith; rule 8, choose to believe that consolation will return *soon*; and rule 9, consideration of God's three reasons for allowing us to undergo desolation.

Rule 10 offers counsel for what to do when we are in a state of consolation: first, we should simply embrace the closeness we feel with God; but second, *we should prepare for future desolation.* Desolation is so powerful because it knocks us on our back *unexpectedly.* But if we know that the normal course of things is to alternate back and forth between consolation and desolation, then we should prepare and strengthen ourselves ahead of time, while we are in consolation—while it's still easy to strengthen ourselves.

For starters, we can prepare for the "lie" that will tempt us in desolation. We know we'll be tempted to break the spiritual resolutions we made during consolation, so before desolation hits we can firm up our resolve to remain true to them when desolation does arrive (rule 5). We know that desolation will attempt to redefine our spiritual past and future, so while in a state of consolation, we can think about our past encounters with God and his faithfulness in our lives and remind ourselves to meditate upon them when desolation comes (rule 6). And we can resolve now, while in consolation, that when desolation arrives we will choose to view our desolation in light of faith, knowing that God is still at work in us in the midst of desolation (rule 7). We can further resolve—when future desolation does hit—that we will choose to believe that consolation will return soon (rule 8). We know that when desolation strikes our inclination will be to believe the opposite (that desolation will last forever), so we have to firm up our resolve now (in consolation) while our spiritual energies are still high.

Further, while in consolation, we could also review Ignatius's fourteen rules, since they are most helpful when they are at our fingertips; in desolation, we certainly won't be inclined to review and meditate upon them. That's why doing so in a state of consolation is good preparation: it increases our ability to understand what is happening in desolation and know how best to counteract it.

Rule 11 gives general counsel for when we are in both consolation and desolation. In consolation, we should try to *humble* ourselves, since our natural bent will be to get inflated and prideful—which makes desolation all the more devastating when it comes upon us unexpectedly. Ignatius's counsel here (while in consolation) is to think about how little we can do when in a state of desolation. This thought helps to bring us back down to earth while we are experiencing the spiritual high of consolation.

Conversely, in a state of desolation, we should try to foster an attitude of *trust* and *confidence*. In effect, we need to *lower* ourselves in consolation and *raise* ourselves in desolation. Ignatius's vision is for us to seek a spiritual equilibrium—*neither too naively high, nor too despairingly low.* By humbling ourselves in consolation and building ourselves up in desolation, we will strike this spiritual balance.

Rules 12–14 are about the tactics of the Evil One. Rule 12 notes that, *in the beginning of temptation*, he is essentially weak; for this reason, we must try to resist temptation early and energetically. The Enemy is likened here to a spoiled child: if confronted early on with strength, the child often gives in; but if allowed to have its own way, the child becomes a terror.[3] So too, the longer we let temptation linger, the stronger the power of the Evil One grows, creating a "snowball effect" that gets bigger and bigger the more it continues to roll.

Rule 13 describes the Enemy's desire for *secrecy*. Ignatius describes the Enemy as like unto a "false lover," someone who attempts to seduce under the darkness of night. If we are spiritually troubled *and* we feel a resistance to speak to a spiritual mentor or counselor, there is a good chance the Enemy is at work—for he loves to work in *secret*.

Rule 14 describes the Enemy as like unto a brigand, scouting out a fortress in order to attack it at its weakest point: thus, *the Enemy will attack us at our weakest and most vulnerable spot.* We

3. Gallagher, *Discernment*, 152.

must, therefore, become aware of our weakest point and seek to fortify it preemptively ahead of time.

This could be as simple as having a sense for what people or situations tend to bring us down into desolation—our triggers and points of vulnerability. If we're aware of this ahead of time, we can seek to counteract this tendency and preemptively strengthen ourselves. Simply considering our most vulnerable spot, and expecting the attack to come there, is already a great gain, since the power of the attack usually lay in its taking us by surprise.

In sum, all of these rules, for Ignatius, are aimed at one goal: to help us overcome desolation. As we get better at overcoming desolation, its grip over us begins to loosen, and the captives are set free. The devil thereby loses his ability to keep us down—and we move from despair to hope and confidence.

This doesn't happen overnight, but the more we can rise above our spontaneous emotional reactions and identify what is happening in the midst of desolation, the more we can take active steps to resist it. Just like virtue, the more practice we get at understanding what is happening in the midst of desolation and taking active steps to resist it, the better we get at resisting—and the more habitual it becomes. That is, as it becomes habit, it becomes easier and easier for us—and thus we grow in our freedom to overcome desolation. Again, this is largely why God allows us to undergo this trial: so that in resisting, we may learn to resist more readily and effectively. Slowly and steadily, then, the devil's grip over us is more and more undone. Even desolation will no longer be able to hold us down—for we will have broken through its lie and only therein does it have any enduring power.

Bibliography

Benedict XVI, Pope. *Jesus of Nazareth.* Vol. 1, *From the Baptism in the Jordan to the Transfiguration.* New York: Doubleday, 2007.

Catechism of the Catholic Church. 2nd ed. Libreria Editrice Vaticana, 1997.

Descartes, Rene. *Discourse on Method and Meditations on First Philosophy.* Trans. Donald A. Cress. Indianapolis: Hackett, 1998.

Erhman, Bart. *How Jesus Became God: The Exaltation of a Jewish Preacher from Galilee.* New York: HarperCollins, 2014.

Evans, Craig A., and N. T. Wright. *Jesus, the Final Days: What Really Happened.* Louisville,: Westminster John Knox, 2009.

Gallagher, Timothy. *Discernment of Spirits: An Ignatian Guide for Everyday Living.* New York: Crossroad, 2005.

Hahn, Scott. *A Father Who Keeps His Promises: God's Covenant Love in Scripture.* Cincinnati: Servant, 1998.

Hofer, Andrew, ed. *Divinization: Becoming Icons of Christ through the Liturgy.* Chicago: Hillenbrand, 2015.

Jenkins, Phillip. *Hidden Gospels: How the Search for Jesus Lost Its Way.* Oxford: Oxford University Press, 2001.

John Paul II, Pope. *Man and Woman He Created Them: A Theology of the Body.* Trans. Michael Waldstein. Boston: Pauline, 2006.

Keener, Craig. *Miracles: The Credibility of the New Testament Accounts.* Vol. 1. Grand Rapids: Baker, 2011.

Kreeft, Peter, and Ronald K. Tacelli. *Handbook of Christian Apologetics: Hundreds of Answers to Crucial Questions.* Downers Grove, IL: Intervarsity, 1994.

Lewis, C. S. *The Great Divorce.* San Francisco: Harper, 2001.

———. *Mere Christianity.* San Francisco: Harper, 2001.

———. *Miracles: A Preliminary Study.* San Francisco: Harper, 2001.

———. *The Screwtape Letters.* San Francisco: HarperCollins, 2001.

Meconi, David, and Carl E. Olsen, eds. *Called to Be the Children of God.* San Francisco: Ignatius, 2016.

Nault, Jean-Charles. *The Noonday Devil: Acedia, the Unnamed Evil of Our Times.* Trans. Michael J. Miller. San Francisco: Ignatius, 2013.

Philippe, Jacques. *Searching for and Maintaining Peace: A Small Treatise on Peace of Heart.* Trans. George and Jannic Driscoll. Staten Island, NY: Society of St. Paul, 2002.

Pitre, Brant. *The Case for Jesus: The Biblical and Historical Evidence for Christ.* New York: Image, 2016.

———. *Jesus and the Jewish Roots of the Eucharist: Unlocking the Secrets of the Last Supper.* New York: Doubleday, 2011.

———. *Jesus and the Last Supper.* Grand Rapids: Eerdmans, 2015.

Scheeben, Matthias Joseph. *The Mysteries of Christianity.* Trans. Cyril Vollert. St. Louis: Herder, 1946.

Snelll, R. J. *Acedia and Its Discontents: Metaphysical Boredom in an Empire of Desire.* Kettering, OH: Angelico, 2015.

Stanley, Scott M., Daniel Trathen, Savanna McCain, and Milt Bryan, *Lasting Promise: A Christian Guide to Fighting for Your Marriage.* San Franciso: Jossey-Bass, 2002.

Swafford, Andrew. *John Paul II to Aristotle and Back Again.* Eugene, OR: Wipf and Stock, 2015.

———. "Laudato Si, Creation & Humanism." June 26, 2015. http://biblestudyforcatholics.com/laudato-si-look-creational-humanism/.

Swafford, Sarah. *Emotional Virtue: A Guide to Drama-Free Relationships.* Denver: Totus Tuus, 2014.

Thomas Aquinas. *Summa Theologiae.* 5 vols. Translated by Fathers of the English Dominican Province. Westminster, MD: Christian Classics, 1981.

Weddell, Sherry A. *Forming Intentional Disciples: The Path to Knowing and Following Jesus.* Huntington, IN: Our Sunday Visitor, 2012.

Wright, N. T. Wright. *Jesus and the Victory of God.* Minneapolis: Fortress, 1996.

———. *The Resurrection of the Son of God.* Minneapolis: Fortress, 2003.

CPSIA information can be obtained
at www.ICGtesting.com
Printed in the USA
LVHW042330050123
736576LV00024B/569